BIBLICAL MONEY DYNAMICS

by David Mallonee

CONTENTS

HEALING THE BREACH

There is a breach that needs to be healed. Too many believers think that God has let them down in their finances. They have faithfully given their tithes and offerings, expecting their finances to be blessed. This never fully occurred and, as a result, some have walked away from an active faith. I sense the Lord saying that it is time to "heal the breach."

Here is the problem which needs addressing: too many Christians have found their reaping disconnected from their sowing. The prophet Haggai addressed this dilemma thousands of years ago when he said:

"You have sown much, and bring in little…" (Haggai 1:6).

How sad. I'm sure the prophet desired to give a different message, but he could not. God was speaking to correct the problem.

I became aware of this breach during the eight years I spent as a pastor. We were learning some very powerful things from the Word of God. We knew that our Heavenly Father had made promises which covered every area of life, including finances. Those promises weren't small either. Phrases like, *"good measure," "pressed down," "shaken together,"* and *"running over,"* and *"not room enough to receive it"* painted a huge picture. How could you not be excited by those words from Scripture? Presented properly, these verses and others

1

like them take expectancy to a very high level.

Some noticed that what they were reading in the Bible, and what they were reading in their checkbooks, were two different things. They remarked, "Pastor, I'm a tither and giver, but what the Bible says should be happening in my finances, and what really is happening, are two different things!" Their reaping was disconnected from their sowing.

Over the past several years there has been an ocean of teaching on *sowing and reaping*. It seems that most of that instruction has emphasized the *sowing* side far more than the reaping side. This is a dominant factor in the disconnect. It is very difficult to find information about how people in the Bible reaped on the offerings they gave. This book addresses that deficit.

The Ways of God

There is a widespread belief that reaping is mostly automatic. You give to the Lord and money begins pouring in from every direction. Much of this mindset comes from an unending use of Luke 6:38 from the King James version:

> *Give and it shall be given to you; good measure, pressed down, and shaken together, and running over, shall men give into your bosom...*
>
> Luke 6:38a, KJV

The context around the verse discusses love, mercy, forgiveness, etc. While money is not directly mentioned, we know the principle applies to finances as well (see Galatians 6:7). The phrase which gets the most attention is, "...*shall men give into your bosom.*" This one excerpt from one translation has produced the idea that after I give others will be inspired to give money to me. It becomes even more established in hearts and minds when ministers share how they have received money through offerings, in the mail, etc.

It is enlightening to read Luke 6:38 from other major translations: New King James, New American Standard, New International, etc. All of those versions omit a couple of words used in the KJV. Here is the verse from the NKJV:

> *Give, and it will be given to you: good measure, pressed down, shaken together, and running over will be put into your bosom. For with the same measure that you use, it will be measured back to you.*

Did you notice any words missing that were in the KJV? The phrase, *"shall men"* is not there. Luke 6:38, in all the translations, makes clear that I will be immensely blessed, but they move me away from expecting someone to walk up and hand me money. This small shift in thinking is vital. It moves me from a passive, waiting-for-men-to-give-me-money-stance, to an active, Bible-based approach.

Our understanding is further complicated when ministers tell us that it will work for us the same way it works for them. I know this is said with the best of intentions, but I believe it to be inaccurate. Our intuition tells us it doesn't work the same for us as it does for a legitimate, full-time minister. The promises are the same to both parties, but the mechanics are different. A measure of relief comes by recognizing this simple fact.

There is a natural bias towards giving money to ministers, and appropriately so. Ministers are called to do things that require significant funding. We want to be a part and so we give towards those projects. It is a blessing to do so. A minister may stand before a large group of people and share a God-given vision. He can use Scriptures which speak of both the responsibility and blessing in giving. When an offering is received under those circumstances, the response will be generous. The minister can urge those listening to visit the book table and purchase materials which will be edifying. He can also enlist the willing to be monthly partners.

All of the above are legitimate means for ministers to receive funds. The money received is for the gift and anointing. It is designed to accomplish kingdom objectives. Those without a call to full-time ministry cannot receive funds by the same *methods*. Ministers live in the "world of offerings"; they give and receive offerings. This may come through in their teaching and sound as though others can receive funds in the same way. My interest was not in how ministers receive money, but how the "butcher, baker, and candlestick maker" receive money.

Consider the case of Joe Plumber. He cannot take up an offering, and there is no natural bias for people to give him money. He does not have a book and tape table. The only monthly partners he has are those with really bad plumbing. God's promises are just as real to him, but the methods will be a little different. This book is dedicated to the average Joe Christian.

Connecting Sowing and Reaping

The Scriptures have much to say on this topic and there are some things which sever the reaping from the sowing. We will be look at those in this book. A prominent factor is a "lack of knowledge" on reaping. The Bible does say that God's people are *destroyed* for a lack of knowledge (Hosea 4:6). So how did people in the Bible make money? How did their finances go to the next level? How did they raise their income? Much of the current teaching about money has spoken only to sowing and has not fully answered those questions.

Miscommunication about money has caused a breach that needs to be healed. In plain English, people gave and the money didn't come in as they heard it would. This break has left some in a spiritually dull state. They are still attending church, going through the motions, but—practically speaking—are backslidden. They are plagued by the thought that if this part of God's Word doesn't work, what about the other parts?

About This Book

I have always believed that financial change begins on the inside. Our Heavenly Father mends something internally which translates into external increase. We need divine order and the peace of God inside which leads to improvement outside. This book is designed in that format. The chapters in the front look at those internal repairs and the chapters toward the back look at the means employed by biblical characters to raise their income. I consider this to be a healthy arrangement.

Our Heavenly Father wants your reaping to equal your sowing. I believe you will find this book one of the most exciting studies you have ever done on biblical finance. Your heart is going to rejoice as you read through this book. I am confident it will begin a change on the inside that won't stop until it has made a lasting change in your checkbook!

CHAPTER ONE

WHY MONEY FLOWS TO SOME PEOPLE AND AWAY FROM OTHERS

W ater is a powerful force. Since the beginning of creation, God has used it to shape and reshape this planet. A small stream may seem to have little significance, but when it combines with other streams, it becomes a mighty river. Anything traveling with that water is virtually unstoppable.

In fact, the life of a river is found in its movement. It must keep traveling onward in order to stay alive. If its flow were to stop, the water would quickly become stagnant and poisoned.

If you waded into a powerful river right now, one of the first things you would notice is the current. It forces you to adjust your footing and balance. You can readily sense where the water is coming from. Obviously, your perspective will be noticeably different, depending on whether you are facing upstream or downstream.

This simple illustration makes a strong point about a Christian's finances. We may, at times, stand in the stream of this world's wealth and watch it flow powerfully away from us. At other times, we may see that same wealth flowing toward us. The difference is one of positioning. Most people show keen interest in learning how to turn so they can face the flow, allowing it to come their way.

Jesus made a particular statement which led me to the river example you have just read. He made this statement more than once. Allow me to quote from the passage which struck me first. Illumination of those words began a turnaround in my own life financially.

> *For whoever has, to him more will be given; but whoever does not have, even what he has will be taken away from him...*

Mark 4:25

In its most basic sense this verse means the person who has something will get more of what he already has, and the person who lacks will lose the little he or she already has.

That direct statement by the Lord runs contrary to what most would think is *fair*. In order to sound fair, the verse would need to read: The one who has something shouldn't get any more because he already has some. The one who doesn't have anything should get something because, Lord knows, he needs it. This revision would be well accepted!

We might wish Jesus had said things differently. It is possible to even be discouraged by His remark, but please don't take that verse the wrong way. Don't think, "I always felt my situation was hopeless; now I know for sure it is 'cause I read it in the Bible." Mark 4:25 is simply expression of a kingdom principle that affects every aspect of life, including money.

Mark 4:25 showcases two distinct sides. There is a side you want to be on and one you don't! Have you decided yet which one you prefer? Of course you have! The moment you read the verse you had a desire to be on the preferred side. If in some facet of your life you have ended up on the adverse side of Mark. 4:25, don't be downcast. It is possible to move to the other position! The grace of God is more than enough to spark a change. The Bible shares portraits of those who experienced major turnarounds financially.

It's that Verse Again

I have given a lot of thought to what Jesus said and how it applies spiritually. This caused me to recall the different seminars and meetings we held as a church. I noticed that regardless of the topic or subject, usually the people who needed those particular services the most were absent.

Perhaps someone came to teach on prayer. Those few members who complained about unanswered prayer the most were usually the ones not there.

Guess who did attend the meetings on prayer? People who regularly prayed, received answers, and were interested in learning how to be more effective. Initially, this reality frustrated me. Understanding Mark 4:25 more fully, I could look at the situation and say, "You know, it's that verse, *'…whoever has, more will be given.'*"

I will never forget one situation as long as I live. A few in the church were having a difficult time locating and retaining a job. Church leaders tried to help them by both prayer and counsel. Then one of the leaders expressed a creative idea. "Pastor," he said, "why don't we have a job seminar? We have conferences on other issues, so why not one on how to find a job? He suggested we teach people how to dress for an interview and how to fill out a job application correctly. We could see to it that everyone's résumé is in order. Simulated interviews can be arranged in order for everyone to be mentally, emotionally, and spiritually prepared to find a job. Let's do everything we can to assist them."

I loved the idea. We prepared spiritually with prayer and naturally by planning. We expected God to give break-throughs. We had our fellow members' interest at heart.

The numerical response was good and the meeting was a success. We had guests from other congregations, but I noted with surprise those who attended. Hardly any of those needing a job attended. Instead, those who came to the job seminar were people who already had jobs. They wanted to learn how to get a better one. All I could say was, "It's that verse—Mark 4:25." "For whoever has, to him more will be given..."

Moving with the Current

I understood Mark 4:25 as a precept that also pertained to finances. I saw that I am either in a position where money is flowing to me or I am turned where money is flowing from me.

What makes me think this verse applies to finances? While it makes a general statement, Jesus states a life principle with application in every realm—spiritual, social, financial, etc. He did not say, "except in the realm of finances." Because He did not exclude money, it is appropriate to explore its implications there as well.

Anyone Can Turn Around

The illumination of Mark 4:25 helped me personally. Even though I was a pastor and making a reasonably good salary, I sensed money was flowing from me. My financial net worth was negative with no turnaround in sight. The outlook could have been very depressing.

At that point, the above realizations began to excite me. I had no enthusiasm for the idea that money was flowing from me. Rather, I knew that both sides of this verse are equally powerful. I was excited that if I changed places in that verse, money could flow to me as powerfully as it had flowed away in the past.

I was experiencing the wrong side of that verse through my own mistakes or maybe through lack of training. I had been there for a long time. I was excited that Spirit-inspired changes would put me on the right side of Jesus' statement.

A river flows in one direction. I can face either upstream or downstream. If I want water to come to me, I do not have to change the direction of the current. Rather, the turn must occur in me as I face a new way.

I cannot alter the principle of Mark 4:25 or deny what Jesus said. What I can do, however, is allow the Holy Spirit to direct and inspire changes in me. His internal work will turn me around and position me on the right side of this verse.

Dealing with the Holes

Dollar amounts are irrelevant. The truth of Mark 4:25 has absolutely nothing to do with how much money a person makes. Rather, its application involves a spiritual principle, such as what the prophet Haggai outlines:

> *Now therefore, thus says the Lord of hosts: "Consider your ways! You have sown much, and bring in little; You eat, but do not have enough; You drink, but you are not filled with drink; You clothe yourselves, but no one is warm; And he who earns wages, earns wages to put into a bag with holes."*

Haggai 1:5-6

The wallets and pocketbooks of today were called money bags in Haggai's time. When Christians ask God for financial help, the focus is typically on God pouring more in the top. The thinking is that more money will solve our financial problems.

What if God looked in our money bag and all He saw was daylight? A huge hole is in the bottom of the pouch. Would it make sense for Him to keep shoveling more in the top?

If God pours $40,000 a year into a holey money bag, how much will be left? Nothing. What if God poured in any amount you could name—how much would remain? Still nothing! My point is that being turned into the flow has little to do with how much money goes in the top. Greater amounts of cash flow might be more fun, but your outcome is still the same.

I have heard from individuals who earning very high incomes. In spite of substantial cash flow, they were having financial difficulty. The remarks they made were familiar: "I don't know where it all went" or, "I don't have much to show for it"; etc. They often had a debt problem as well. Such stories illustrate that money can be flowing from us, even if our income is large. If I have a hole in my money bag and God increases the amount of money pouring in, I might end up with complications on a larger scale.

The Holy Spirit's work is to initially focus on the bottom of the bag. The wisdom of God leads a believer to understand what created the hole. The next step is to find His direction to effect the repair. As the "hole" is mended you will find that God has been providing better for you than realized. Second, you will discover that it is easier to ask God to pour more into the top when you know that you have repaired the opening in the bottom.

Habits and Actions

Before we can turn around financially, we need to discern what is creating the flow from us. The Lord put on my heart two distinct themes.

The first area is what I call "Habits and Actions." The second group is "Attitudes and Motives." My response to these two groups puts me in a position of either money flowing to me powerfully or of money flowing from me powerfully.

The Book of Proverbs is the greatest work on finances ever written and deserves our utmost attention. It often speaks of normal, human impulses that when allowed to be out of control, become actions that squander the provision God has already made. They will drain us to a place of lack. I want you to keep this in mind as you proceed through this book. There is another chapter totally devoted to the subject of money and character flaws. That chapter looks in depth at Solomon's discussion of the two classifications mentioned above. It is a life changing topic.

Financial Turning Points

Allow me to define a turning point. It is not something that occurs because the price of gasoline rises twenty cents a gallon. While that may pinch a little, it is not a turning point. A few hours of overtime in next week's paycheck is not a turning point either. It is certainly nice, but still not in the league of a turning point.

A turning point is a clear reversal of fortune. It is not an everyday occurrence, nor do we need such to happen regularly. Since most of us begin financially on the wrong side of Mark 4:25, we only want one turning point!

Turning points in Scripture were preceded by strong spiritual activity. A biblical figure might be positioned where money was flowing from them. They would then have an experience with God. He might speak a word of great magnitude or provide a revelation. The impact was internal change. The exchange turned them around on the inside and money began flowing to them. Let's look at a clear example of this in the life of Job.

Job's Drastic Turnaround

Job indeed provides an excellent example. As the book that bears his name begins, Job had money flowing to him powerfully. He was not merely a rich man; he was the richest man in the East (Job 1:3). Job appeared set for life; he reminds me of that secular saying which has roots in Mark 4:25 (The rich get richer and the poor get poorer). We have all heard that saying and know it by heart. That secular saying is not the full truth, however. In order to be accurate, it requires modification; *Yes, the rich get richer and the poor get poorer, unless there is a change!*

A change was coming toward Job. Even though the outlook was good, strong spiritual activity was on the horizon.

That activity begins in Job 1:8 where the book's namesake is the subject of a debate between God and the devil. Certainly a person being discussed at that level would qualify as powerful activity. As a result of those consultations, Satan became the prime mover of an onslaught against Job. He had few, if any, defenses against that offensive. (Remember Job was probably the first book of the Bible written and at the moment there were no covenants to help Job). He bemoaned not having a mediator between himself and God. Today we have the new covenant with all its power, the name of Jesus, and there is a mediator between us and God, the man Christ Jesus (I Timothy 2:5). The assault on Job created a turning point, including a financial one.

When money began flowing away from him, Job went from being the richest man in the East to one of the poorest. For approximately nine months, Job remained in that state. He became angry, chiding the Lord for treating him unjustly (Job 9:28-35) and cursing the day of his birth (Job 3). Job relied on his own righteousness to sustain him, (see Job 27:6). These attitudes and actions are not expressions of righteousness and became a stronghold in Job.

His friends offered their help and gave their opinions as to why Job was having these problems. They presented explanations based on human understanding, but human wisdom cannot deliver us.

Men did not have the answer for Job. The story does not end there, however. Job 38:1 says, "Then the Lord answered Job out of the whirlwind…." God spoke clearly to Job. It is an expression of immense spiritual activity.

The essence spoken was, "Job, go take a bath, put on some clean clothes, and then come back and answer Me like a man." Those words seem strong for a man who has just lost everything, but the Lord was speaking to Job on a personal level. As Job complied, the Lord continued with reproof and instruction.

Job had fallen into a stronghold: he was held by the power of his own anger and self-righteousness. He was locked in and the money was locked out. Those strong words from God were attacking the stronghold in Job. God was telling Job the truth. I know it was difficult for Job to hear them, but those words were pulling apart that stronghold. Weak works will not break strongholds; it takes strong words to break strongholds.

The force of God's word gave Job a new level of insight. He had a deeper revelation than ever before and that set the stage for his turnaround:

> I have heard of you by the hearing of the ear, but now my eyes see you…

> Job 42:5

Job speaks of having a "head knowledge" about God, but this latest experience has opened his eyes to "see" into the spiritual realm. Financial turning points begin in the spiritual realm.

We think that if we only had a little more money every month, our finances would be better. Yet we actually need something more substantial. *We need God to tell us the truth.* God told Job the truth and the stronghold came down. This spiritual exchange provided a financial turning point. In Job 42:6 Job repents, which means to turn around. He changed on the inside and was set free.

Job's repentance gives us some very important insight.

16

Not all financial problems are solved by giving. A great many financial problems are solved by *repentance. (Well heavens to Betsy!)* A few years back I was ministering in a church and during the Sunday evening service the Spirit of the Lord led us to a place of repentance. A lady present felt led to repent over some financial matters. She had felt bad concerning them, but feeling bad and actually repenting are two different things.

The very next evening she had a financial testimony to share. You see, her husband had left her a couple of years prior and she was thrown into financial chaos. She received a gift of $16,000 which was supposed to be used in paying down her debt. The gift came in increments over a period of time and she would put the money in her checking account. Well, the money ended up going for things other than her debt, and of course she felt bad. She had exercised poor stewardship and been untrue to her word. That Sunday evening she actually repented for her error.

She had been trying to sell her house in hopes of using the equity to pay off the debts, but it simply refused to sell. On Monday morning she received a contract to sell the house at her asking price and that was her testimony. She repented over unwise stewardship and the next day the Father opened the door for her house to sell. Do you see a connection?

Job 42:10 then says:

> And the Lord restored Job's losses when he prayed for his friends. Indeed the Lord gave Job twice as much as he had before.

Job had turned around in his finances by first turning around inside. Money flowed to him as powerfully, if not more powerfully, than it had earlier. Job would probably have been happy to return to the same financial level as before the trial. But God made him twice as rich! Now consider Job 42:11:

> Then all his brothers, all his sisters, and all those who had been his acquaintances before, came to him and ate food with him in his house; and they consoled him and comforted him for all the adversity that the Lord had brought upon him. Each one gave him a piece of silver and each a ring of gold.

Where were these folks when Job really needed them? A little money and a little gold would certainly have been nice six months earlier. When Job lost everything and was broke, no one brought him money or gold. Now God starts making him twice as rich, and friends begin bringing money and gold. Doesn't this seem backwards? Job's experience illustrates the verse emphasized at the beginning of this chapter, Mark 4:25: "For whoever has, to him more will be given; but whoever does not have, even what he has will be taken from him."

I believe Job's friends did not offer him money and gold earlier because Job was crosswise to that principle. Now that a breakthrough has occurred in the spirit, God could bless him and make him twice as rich as he was before. His friends were also free to bring money and gold.

Job shifted to the right side of the principle in Mark 4:25 because of a word from God. It changed him on the inside and delivered external results. This is part of the reason the Bible says that God's word is to be *"more desired than gold"* (Psalm 19:10). Anything "more precious than gold" can also deliver the gold!

Joseph Also Turned into the Flow

Certain events in Joseph's life also help us understand about turning into the flow. Psalm 105:16-18 reads:

> *Moreover He called for a famine in the land; He destroyed all the provision of bread. He sent a man before them—Joseph—who was sold as a slave. They hurt his feet with fetters, he was laid in irons.*

Joseph was sent to Egypt by his brothers and sold as a slave. Later he was thrown into prison for a crime he did not commit. A Hebrew in an Egyptian prison would feel totally hopeless. Joseph was locked into a future that seemed to have no way out.

I liken Joseph's tangible prison to the financial prison we can find ourselves in. It requires only a few things piling up, and before we know it, we are trapped. A few mistakes, a couple of mishaps, a bad business decision, and there we are. Maybe we have hit the peak of our earning potential and are trapped by the rising cost of living. Our financial situation can seem a prison just as real as Joseph's.

Joseph's story would be sad if not for the next word: *until.* That word contains much hope. Psalm 105:19 continues, "Until the time that his word came to pass…." The King James Version says, "Until the time that *his word came* (emphasis added)." Joseph was in prison until a word came from God. That word set Joseph free, broke him out of prison, and freed him from his shackles. Whole new horizons were opened up. It made things possible that were impossible before.

If I am in a financial prison, I need the same experience. I need a word from God of such magnitude and power that it sets me free from prison and open up whole new horizons. Things previously impossible will become possible.

This word did more than set Joseph free. Verse 19 continues, "…The word of the Lord tested him." Translated, the word "tested" also means "to refine." God's word to Joseph not only set him free, it also purified and refined him. It made this human vessel of higher quality, making him more useful. God had plans for Joseph that included being the prime minister of Egypt. When his brothers came to buy grain during the famine, Joseph could have taken revenge. But the word had so purified him that he refused to retaliate. Naturally, he did have some fun with them first (Genesis 42-44).

When Joseph revealed himself to his brothers, he made a statement that sounds as if it belongs in the New Testament. It speaks volumes. In Genesis 45:7, he said, "And God sent me…to save your lives by a great deliverance." Joseph brought life, he brought deliverance, and he cared for his brothers. Are not these actions precisely what the New Testament Church is supposed to do?

In Egypt, Joseph experienced one of the largest wealth transfers that has ever taken place. The Scriptures below reveal the magnitude.

> *Joseph collected all the money that was to be found in Egypt and Canaan in payment for the grain they were buying, and he brought it to Pharaoh's palace. When the money of the people of Egypt and Canaan was gone, all Egypt came to Joseph and said, "Give us food. Why should we die before your eyes? Our money is used up." "Then bring your livestock, since your money is gone." So they brought their livestock to Joseph, and he gave them food in exchange for their horses, their sheep and goats,*

> *their cattle and donkeys…. They came to him the fol-*
> *lowing year and said, "We cannot hide from our lord*
> *the fact that since our money is gone and our live-*
> *stock belongs to you, there is nothing left for our*
> *lord except our bodies and our land. Why should we*
> *perish before your eyes-we and our land as well?*
> *Buy us and our land in exchange for food"…So*
> *Joseph bought all the land in Egypt for Pharaoh…*
> *because the famine was too severe for them. The land*
> *became Pharaoh's.*
>
> Genesis 47:14-20, NIV

The typical person receiving that much wealth would tend to forget God's overall purpose. The temptations of mammon could be overwhelming. But the word to Joseph had purified him and burned God's purpose into his heart. He remembered the divine aim was to bring life, deliverance, and to care for his brothers.

God could trust Joseph with that much money. Joseph had been purified to the extent that he would release money at the proper time to bring life, deliverance, and to care for his brothers. What about Joseph's standard of living? It improved along the way. He enjoyed the best of Egypt. He lived in a palace instead of a prison; he wore Pharaoh's ring and rode in the second chariot of Pharaoh (see Genesis 41:42-43). It could be said that God forced him to accept a higher standard of living. The Lord opened the door and he stepped through.

In Conclusion

Matthew 6:33 presents a balance. Seeking first the Kingdom of God addresses my motives and calls them to the highest possible level. Seeking His righteousness brings His character into my habits and actions; I am to permit His righteousness to come from the inside to the outside. Doing so can not only make me prosper spiritually, but also financially. As transformations occur in my motives and impulses, I become a better steward of the resources God entrusts to me. This enables me to safely experience an improved standard of living.

Certain attitudes and motives can disqualify us from handling God's resources on a larger scale. Undisciplined impulses diminish the provision God has already made. Each one of us needs a Job/Joseph experience. We can look to the Lord for a word in due season. We can look for a word with divine force that will start breaking us out, ripping apart strongholds, and opening new horizons.

The effect will be a burning away of unscriptural attitudes and motives. The purposes of God will be sealed in our heart and we will experience an increased desire to release provision for those purposes. Our standard of living can go up along the way.

In the lives of Job and Joseph, a clear word from God brought a financial turning point. If this happened for them under the Old Covenant, how much more so for us who have a new and better covenant (Hebrews 8:6)?

Prepare to hear. Believe to hear. Expect to hear.

CHAPTER 2

MONEY AND CHARACTER FLAWS

This chapter builds on the part of Chapter One that raised the point of attitudes and motives. There is a relationship in Scripture between our money and character flaws. Character flaws can reach a point where they negatively impact our financial situation.

Here is an important point about money and character flaws. God is so good that He will allow us to have some of both. We can have some money and some character flaws. However, He will not condone us having a lot of both. If we desire to see an increase in our money, be prepared for the Heavenly Father to purge or diminish some character flaw. If we permit a significant rise in character flaws, there can be a forfeiture of finances.

Haggai 1:6 is a verse I use a great deal as it expresses the three kinds of financial problems people can have. Let's look at that verse again:

> You have sown much, and bring in little; You eat, but do not have enough; You drink, but you are not filled with drink; You clothe yourselves, but no one is

warm; And he who earns wages, Earns wages to put into a bag with holes.

The end of the verse paints a very vivid picture. It depicts wage-earners putting their income into a money bag with holes. This is imagery, of course, but it lets us know that there are things which can drain our finances. It is a godly challenge to discern the reason for the loss.

A most helpful tool is the Book of Proverbs. Solomon wrote this book under the unction and anointing of the Spirit. He covered many topics in the book, but a major focus is on finances. Solomon taps his vast experience with large sums of money to help us. He shares insights which will give us an advantage in handling our money. We can absorb his words and profit accordingly.

Woven throughout Proverbs are multiple verses that show a cause-and-effect relationship pertaining to income. The summary is that if we allow certain habits, actions, or attitudes to prevail, our finances will suffer. These character flaws will drag us toward poverty and lack. Here is a sample of those messages:

- If you do this, you will lose money…
- If this action affects your life, money will go from you to a stranger…
- If this impulse is out of control in you, it will give you poverty.

I urge you not to discount the wisdom that comes from Solomon. The verses we will look at contain the "secret" to prosperity. I will share now with you that deep truth. The secret to prosperity is, *avoid poverty!* Solomon conveys that if I avoid the pitfalls that drain our money, by default we will do fairly well.

I have listed below twenty such verses. It is my hope that you will read and meditate these over the time to come. The grace of God will use these verses to effect a change in our behavior.

I have broken down our focus verses into three categories for convenience sake. Those three categories are: moral mistakes, financial mistakes, and work habits. I'm sure these verses could be broken down several different ways, but these three seem to work well. I'm going to list each category with its corresponding verses one at a time.

Moral Mistakes[1]

- **Immorality** (5:10)—Strangers shall be filled with your wealth…(also 6:26)
- **Money by wickedness** (10:3)—The Lord casts away the substance of the wicked…
- **Troubling your family** (11:39)—Shall inherit the wind…
- **Refusing correction** (13:18)—Poverty and shame will come to him…
- **Covering sins** (28:13)—Shall not prosper…
- **Not hearing the poor** (21:13)—Shall cry, but not be heard…
- **Loving pleasure or wine** (21:17)—Shall be a poor man…
- **Gluttony** (23:21)—Shall come to poverty…
- **Vain companions/chasing fantasies** (NIV) (28:19)—Shall have poverty…

---

1 Some of this material on the Proverbs was drawn from Bill Gothard's *Men's Manual*, Volume II, Revised Edition, June 1984, 3rd Printing. (Oak Brook, IL.: Institute in Basic Life Principles).

Let's take a look at a few of the Moral Mistakes listed above. Top on the list has to be immorality. This topic would include adultery, fornication, and anything that is a sexual perversion. The Book of Proverbs says much on this subject in the first few chapters. The warnings given cover everything from the eternal and spiritual consequences (2:16-22) to the financial ramifications (see above).

Another notable item listed above is "troubling your family". If an individual brings shame and expense (through foolishness) to their family, they risk losing some "inheritance" directly or indirectly. Those type of actions are bad seed and will produce a losing crop. If you have brought some type of trouble to your family, it will be necessary for you to repent to God and to them. Our Heavenly Father can recover and restore those fractured relationships. The first commandment with promise was about "honoring our father and mother" and the Apostle Paul emphasized it in Ephesians 6:1-3:

Children, obey your parents in the Lord, for this is right. Honor your father and mother, which is the first commandment with promise: that it may be well with you and you may live long on the earth.

Being in right relationship with your family has powerful promise spiritually and otherwise, including your financial state.

I want to take a look at one more from the above list, "refusing correction." The NKJV uses the word "disdains" and a footnote in the Holman NKJV uses the term "ignores." This is speaking about an attitude. This approach rejects correction on almost any level and has financial consequences.

As Christians we are under the legitimate authority of the Lord Jesus Christ and are "bought with a price" (I Corinthians 6:19-20). God's Word is the place of final appeal. In Hebrews 13:7 the writer admonishes us to receive correction that comes from the clear message of scripture and the fruit of a godly life. Here are his words:

> *Remember those who rule over you, who have spoken the word of God to you, whose faith follow, considering the outcome of their conduct.*

When a fellow believer brings a clear concern to you from the Word of God about something you are doing, check your attitude. Do not "disdain" legitimate correction. Look carefully at the Scripture and the practice in question. If we discard a clear message from the Bible, we're not disobeying an individual, we are disobeying the Author of Scripture, God Himself. No wonder that there will be spiritual as well as financial ramifications.

Financial Mistakes

- **Not being generous** (11:24-25)—Tends toward poverty…
- **Money without labor** (13:11)—It shall be diminished…
- **Unwise use of credit** (22:7)—Borrower is the servant to the lender…
- **Giving to the rich** (22:16)—Shall come to want…
- **Get rich quick schemes** (28:22)—Poverty shall come… 13:11, 21:5, 20:21, 28:20)
- **Lack of planning** (24:3-4 LB)—Any enterprise is built by wise planning…

Our second area from the Proverbs is what I call "Financial Mistakes." These are monetary decisions which will make us poorer. They are "poor" decisions in every sense of the word.

A few years ago I made a trip to our local veterinarian. I was there to buy vaccine for some calves that my sons were raising to sell for profit. Upon my arrival there was a vehicle parked in front that was in very bad shape. Inside was a couple that had brought four small dogs to the vet for some shots, etc. The couple looked as if they were hurting financially and yet their bill for those four dogs was $87. My bill for the vaccine was $15.

In my heart I heard the Lord whisper that this couple was making a "poor" decision. They could have used that $87 elsewhere and yet their decision to have that many pets was costing them much needed money. The $15 I spent was recovered when the calves were sold.

We all have made some "poor" decisions in our time. Proverbs will help us to reduce these and in their place we will make some "rich" decisions. I cannot emphasize enough how helpful it will be to meditate the profiled twenty verses.

This reminds me of a testimony I received several years ago. I had spoken at a particular church and in that one service I encouraged those present to read and meditate the aforementioned Proverbs. A few months later a couple wrote me to tell me that the time they had spent in Proverbs had already started turning around their finances. They were so confident in the change that for the first time in their life they had ordered "Christian witness" checks. They had never used checks with a Christian message before as they did not want their financial mess to reflect poorly on the Lord. A bounced check with "Smile—God Loves You" on its face is a bad witness. I admired their sensitivity.

They attributed their progress to the time they spent meditating those financial Proverbs. They believed it mended something internal and that repair showed up in their checkbook. That word will transmit the same power into our situation.

The first item listed under Financial Mistakes is "not being generous." This is a financial decision and means we are not adequately distributing money to advance kingdom purposes. This chokes off the flow in our direction and slides us toward poverty. The Bible doesn't make many promises to stingy people.

On the other hand, there are ample promises to those who will distribute resources to meet the legitimate needs of others, such as this passage from Luke 12:

> [42]*And the Lord said, Who then is that faithful and wise steward, whom his master will make ruler over his household, to give them their portion of food in due season?* [43]*Blessed is that servant whom his master will find so doing when he comes.* [44]*Truly, I say to you that he will make him ruler over all that he has.*

The above verses say that if I will give to meet the needs of others, the master will place me in charge of everything he owns. Think about that in relationship to our Master and the magnitude of what He owns. As He places us in charge of more of His possessions, imagine the impact it will have on our finances. Our standard of living will be forced to go higher.

Another financial mistake I'd like to comment on is the one entitled "Unwise use of credit." We live in an era in which it is incredibly easy to accumulate debt. We see both undisciplined borrowers and undisciplined lenders.

What can we do to be delivered from this trap?

The first thing to do is read and study what God's Word says about debt. This will build up our consciousness on the matter from God's perspective. Since borrowing has been made so easy, we may turn to the lender before turning to the Lord. We will benefit if we can stand stronger and ask God to work things out in a way that avoids our borrowing. In addition to Proverbs 22:7, let me suggest you spend some time in the passage found in Deuteronomy 28:1-14.

Modern financial counseling, and even the Bible, does not treat all debt the same. Most teachers on the subject do not have a problem with someone borrowing moderately for a house or for a business. This may not be the best or highest, but these assets will appreciate or produce income. The prophet instructed the widow in II Kings 4:1-7 to borrow some vessels to use in making money. Check out the passage:

> *A certain woman of the wives of the sons of the prophets cried out to Elisha, saying, "Your servant my husband is dead, and you know that your servant feared the Lord. And the creditor is coming to take my two sons to be his slaves." So Elisha said to her, "What shall I do for you? Tell me, what do you have in the house?" And she said, "Your maidservant has nothing in the house but a jar of oil." Then he said, "Go, borrow vessels from everywhere, from all your neighbors—empty vessels; do not gather just a few. And when you have come in, you shall shut the door behind you and your sons; then pour it into all those vessels, and set aside the full ones." So she went from him and shut the door behind her and her sons, who brought [the] [vessels] to her; and she poured [it] out.*

Now it came to pass, when the vessels were full, that she said to her son, "Bring me another vessel." And he said to her, "[There] [is] not another vessel." So the oil ceased. Then she came and told the man of God. And he said, "Go, sell the oil and pay your debt; and you [and] your sons live on the rest."

The bottom line is for every person to be fully persuaded in their own mind (Romans 14:5b) as they deal with debt. There are many positive reasons to have a vision for lower debt. Debt can get so high that it disconnects our reaping from our sowing. Lower debt levels will increase the financial power and opportunity we can access.

Proverbs 24:3-4 from the Living Bible deserves a good look. It deals with the "planning" aspect of finances and the positive consequences it brings. Take a look:

Any enterprise is built by wise planning, becomes strong through common sense, and profits wonderfully by keeping abreast of the facts.

Christians need to study biblical money management. We must learn how to budget as well as make wise purchases. These are two of the best things you could ever do financially. As the adage goes, "When my outgo exceeds my income, my upkeep becomes my downfall." The discipline of spending less than we earn will make us financially successful.

Work Habits

- **Sleeping too much** (6:11)—So shall poverty come…
- **Lack of diligence** (10:4)—He becomes poor…
- **Slothfulness** (19:15)—Shall suffer hunger…

- **Talking too much** (14:23)—Tends only to penury (lack)…
- **Chasing fantasies** (28:19, NIV)—Will have poverty…

It is interesting that Solomon did not overlook the topic of Work Habits. Any divine financial inspiration will be stymied by poor work habits. Joseph received a tremendous revelation when the Lord showed him seven years of plenty followed by seven years of famine (Genesis 41:29-31). In practical terms Joseph knew the direction of grain prices for the next fourteen years. That type of information is unbelievably lucrative. He proposed a strategy to take advantage of that information which was accepted by Pharaoh.

A fact that could be overlooked is that Genesis 41:46 tells us that Joseph traveled all over the land of Egypt implementing his plan. This would suggest that there were some early mornings, some late nights, and some long chariot rides down many dusty roads. In other words, he worked very diligently in cooperation with the insight he was given. Any benediction will need a good effort to succeed.

The Proverbs listed above yield a broad perspective of diligence. One detraction from diligence is "sleeping too much." Other verses in Proverbs speak of the excuses a slothful person gives for oversleeping and they are quite amusing (22:13). Naturally, a person should get a healthy amount of sleep. Being rested and focused will allow us to be our most productive. But it is over the line for laziness to cause anyone to spend an unusually large amount of hours dozing. *Poverty shall come!*

I want to take a moment to discuss one of the other things listed above, *chasing fantasies*. This is similar to the warnings we studied concerning a get-rich-quick mentality. We have all met someone who is constantly working on a big deal that never quite happens. It's always just around the corner.

This is relevant to committed Christians because we know from Scripture that God gives visions (Acts 2:17). There is a fine line between vision and fantasy. They both look alike in the beginning. But there is a huge difference between them, as one will come to pass and the other never will.

There are three things to look at in deciding if something is a vision or fantasy. We have the witness of the Spirit inside, the Word of God, and confirming counsel from the brethren. The optimal situation is for all three to line up.

First, we sense a leading inside and believe God is giving us direction. Hopefully our prayer life and maturity has taught us to discern the genuine leading of the Spirit. Even when we are sure God is speaking to us, it is always right to check what we are sensing against the Bible. No leading from God would ever violate a clear mandate from Scripture. Is the leading consistent with biblical principle?

Finally, we can receive confirming counsel from those who are close to us and over us in the Lord. If we are surrounded by those who have yielded their lives to the Lord and have no agenda, their input about any decision can be priceless. Be careful not to spurn this input.

Have you ever met someone who had a "wild" idea, but everyone around them tried to explain to them why it wouldn't work? There is a verse which fits that scenario in Proverbs 26:

> *16The lazy man is wiser in his own eyes Than seven*

men who can answer sensibly.

The sluggard simply will not receive any counsel which is contrary to his own ideas. I find this especially to be true when people are pursuing some sort of financial scheme. They have stumbled onto an easy way to make money (so they think) and everyone else is too close-minded to understand. In spite of loving warnings, they forge ahead only to get clobbered one more time. All that heartache could have been avoided if they knew how to accommodate good counsel.

I Work Because...

A. Adam sinned and now we have to work.

B. I have bills.

C. Work is a high calling for a believer.

I hope your answer was C. Work is not a result of the fall. Adam was commissioned by the Lord to work before he sinned. Note this verse from Genesis 2:

> 15 *Then the Lord God took the man and put him in the garden of Eden to tend and keep it.*

Work is not to be viewed as unspiritual. It is a calling on our life. The workplace is where most of us will intersect with lost men and women. **We do not work simply to pay bills. The fruit of our labor allows us to help meet the needs of others.** Note Ephesians 4:28:

> *Let him who stole steal no longer, but rather let him labor, working with [his] hands what is good, that he may have something to give him who has need.*

Being employed does not make you a second class Christian. Don't think that if you were really believing God you wouldn't need this job. God has chosen our vocation as the primary, but not the only means to meet our financial needs. Work is something God blesses, as He promised to bless the work of our hands (Deuteronomy 28:12). Think about that as you leave the house for work; I'm about to do something that God will bless.

Attitudes and Motives

It is equally important that we address attitudes and motives. These are the main scriptural concern in relationship to money. A motive is the underlying reason we do a thing. Judas gave Jesus a kiss in the garden, but it was not to show affection. The underlying reason was betrayal.

Misdirected motives, or underlying reasons, can negatively impact our finances. **Even the powerful force of giving can be derailed by giving with the wrong motives.** Paul warns that **giving for reasons other than love can delete any harvest.** Notice this verse from I Corinthians 13:

> *3And though I bestow all my goods to feed the poor, and though I give my body to be burned, but have not love, it profits me nothing.*

Make no mistake about it; people can give for any number of reasons other than love. They can give under manipulation or they can give out of greed. These situations risk a loss of harvest. The Scripture calls us to the highest possible motive, giving for love's sake.

The Book of James was written to Christians who were desiring more material things. They were asking God for them unsuccessfully. James addresses the cause: they were extreme in their greed. We may not be consumed with greed as they were, but there still could be room for the Holy Spirit to do some adjustment in our lives. Here's the key verse from James chapter 4:

> 3 *You ask and do not receive, because you ask amiss, that you may spend [it] on your pleasures.*

I like this verse in the New American Standard. It says, "You ask and do not receive, because you ask with *wrong motives*... (emphasis added)." The passage teaches me that impure motives short circuit answers to prayer, including financial ones. There appear to be little attitudes or motives, which if I cling to, will disqualify me from handling God's resources on a larger scale. Below are three motives the Bible seeks to cleanse us from:

- The love of money...I Timothy 6:10
- Serving money...Matthew 6:24
- Focusing on luxury...Luke 12:16-21

The Bible teaches that Christians can experience increase. However, with a little human greed mixed in, that pure Bible message becomes a strange concoction. Greed can twist the outlook of the heart. **God must do such a work in our heart that we genuinely put the Kingdom of God first. At the same time we can recognize that God does not mind if our standard of living goes up in the process.**

The Upside to Attitudes and Motives

The New Testament teaching about finances is a blend of warnings and promises. I must not neglect one or the other. I must heed the warnings and embrace the promises. I need to be sensitive to both sides of the equation.

> By humility and the fear of the Lord are riches and honor and life...
>
> Proverbs 22:4

Humility is an attitude; the fear of the Lord is a motive. If the right attitudes and motives find a place in my heart, then instead of riches, honor, and life flowing from me, they can flow to me.

Matthew 6:33 sums up much of what I've said about habits and actions, as well as attitudes and motives:

> But seek first the kingdom of God and His righteousness, and all these things shall be added to you.

"Seek first the Kingdom of God" means having God's interests at heart. Whatever is important to Him must be important to us. In addition, I am to seek His righteousness, i.e., permit His righteousness to control my actions and habits. This dynamic combination brings a lift to my finances.

A Holy Pattern

There is an overall pattern in Scripture where God deals with character flaws before He prospers a person. There are many passages we could turn to and for starters I have chosen Proverbs 8:20-21:

> I traverse the way of righteousness, in the midst of the paths of justice, that I may cause those who love me to inherit wealth, that I may fill their treasuries.

The King James Version reads, "In the midst of the paths of *judgment*" (Proverbs 8:20b, emphasis added). The same idea appears in the New Testament where we are called to judge ourselves (see I Corinthians 11:31-32). According to these verses, the wisdom of God will lead us to the point where we examine ourselves. Self-judgment and repentance paves the way to receiving a fuller treasury.

We should desire for the Lord to purge our character flaws before we experience increase. An internal change is essential as we turn "in the stream" and money begins flowing toward us. Your financial stream may be a trickle now, but as you apply some of the things written in this book, it will expand. You will want your feet planted on a solid foundation to prevent being swept away.

Here are a few brief examples of some in the Word who experienced what I'm saying. Jacob found himself broke (Genesis 32:10) because he engaged in his own personal get-rich-quick scheme. His strategy involved taking advantage of his brother at a weak moment to secure the birthright (Genesis 25:29-34) and deceiving his father (Genesis 27:18-29). He miscalculated the depth of his brother's anger and was compelled to flee (Genesis 27:41-44). His scheme blew up and he was forced across the Jordan river with very little in possessions.

Most of Genesis 28 is about Jacob's visitation from the Lord. He has a powerful divine encounter that signals the beginning of a change in Jacob. Later God changed his name from Jacob (supplanter) to Israel (prince of God). This visitation and the internal change it wrought prepared him for very large financial blessings (Genesis 30:43).

Another example we have already covered thoroughly is from Job. In Job chapters 38-42 we have God speaking distinctly to Job. The repentance and change in Job allowed for his financial status to double relative to his previous prosperity.

Hopefully these words will cause an expectancy for God to deal with us. We should long for the correction of the Lord. Our highest and best will be the end result. Perhaps when we are praying for money, what we really need is the fire of God which burns away impurities and leaves only the pure metal.

May God send His Holy fire to each of our lives!

CHAPTER 3

MONEY WISDOM FROM I TIMOTHY 6

I have lived as a committed Christian for over twenty-five years. In those years I have been a part of a stream of Christianity which has not been afraid to talk about money. I have probably heard hundreds of sermons about money. That is a very good thing for the most part.

However, in all those messages, there is a major passage in the New Testament dealing with money from which I had not heard a message. I myself had never taught from these verses. How is that possible? It would be like hearing hundreds of messages on salvation and none of them using John 3:16!

I believe the reason that passage is seldom used is because a couple of the verses do not fit our theological picture. In cases like this our theological picture needs to change and if we do change, we will be blessed both inside and out. This forsaken passage has some of the best information available for those who want to make progress in their financial life.

Financial Peace

Those of us who believe that God that wants to do good things in our finances don't quite know what to do with the passage we find in I Timothy 6:6-17. It can be puzzling, especially if perceived as calling for the status quo financially. The human heart yearns to improve their situation; it is a God-given desire.

The passage outlines some of the battles concerning money. Paul shares two vital elements every Christian needs in order to achieve financial victory. In the kingdom of God we approach money much differently than a non-Christian. A message on "How the Wicked Prosper" will not do us any good. We must move forward in a manner consistent with kingdom principles.

Let's look at some key monetary verses from I Timothy 6:6-17:

Now godliness with contentment is great gain… (v. 6)

And having food and clothing with these we shall be content. But those who desire to be rich fall into temptation and a snare, and into many foolish and harmful lusts which drown men in destruction and perdition. For the love of money is a root of all kinds of evil, for which some have strayed from the faith and pierced themselves through with many sorrows… (v. 8-10)

Command those who are rich in this present age not to be haughty, nor to trust in uncertain riches, but in the living God, who gives us richly all things to enjoy… (v. 17)

I see Paul making three main points in this passage. I will outline those points and then proceed to discuss them in more detail.

- Godly character plus contentment (peace) leads to increase…
- Don't desire (long) to be rich…
- It's OK to be rich…

In the first point, drawn from verse 6, Paul makes clear that godly character is essential to financial improvement. It makes sense that godliness (being like God) would help our finances. **Growing in His wisdom and ways will improve every part of our life, including money.** Godly character will save us thousands upon thousands of dollars over our lifetime. It has saved us thousands of dollars on addictions and the treatments necessary for recovery. Godly character has saved us money in ways too numerous to count. This money saved is a powerful foundation for a good financial future.

The main reason there wasn't much teaching on verse 6 in my circles is another word Paul used: *contentment*. That word bugs us. It sounds like God wants us to settle for the status quo. Nothing could be further from the truth.

Paul is addressing the material lust which dwells in the fallen nature of man. Material lust wants everything but cannot be satisfied by anything. This drive will never be satisfied with material things or money, but still calls for more! Material lust compels its victims to find their identity in material things. Most New Testament Scriptures on money address this internal spiritual battle. If we win this battle, it sets the stage for future financial improvement.

Material lust will compel us to constantly overspend and drive us deeply into debt. This pattern will deprive us of the capital needed to invest and make profits. A pattern from the Bible is that God would bring an opportunity along and the individual involved would add money to the equation. A harvest would result. It is important that we not allow material lust to deprive us of needed resources when God brings an opportunity our way. A Christian brother who was a bank officer said there were times he could have bought a dollar for fifty cents, but had no money available to take advantage of the opportunity. (His ship came in and he was at the airport!) God tried to help him reap, but his lack of stewardship prohibited progress.

Paul urges us to turn the fire hose of "contentment" on the flame of material lust. A word compatible with contentment is "peace." The peace of God will turn off that fire. Our finances can be in one of two conditions: high or low. When my money is tight, I need the peace of God in the situation. This is the same peace I will need when my finances improve. **While my financial picture will fluctuate, the peace about it should be constant.**

Contentment should not be confused with complacency. Complacency is an unseemly attitude for a believer. We should apply every gifting diligently in the financial realm. One facet of contentment is not increasing our standard of living until the Lord gives us the green light to do so. He will give us a witness of peace when it is time to step up. Contentment should not be confused with giving up financially. Rather, it is about waiting for God to open the door and then stepping through. It doesn't try to force the door open.

The Wuest[1] translation replaces contentment with, "inward self-sufficiency which is its natural accompaniment." **Christian maturity realizes that no amount of material**

1 *The New Testament: An Expanded Translation* by Kenneth S. Wuest. Wm B. Eerdmans Publishing Co., 1961.

things can meet the biggest need in my life; it also realizes that all of the needs in my life will be met through a vital relationship with our Heavenly Father!

Godly Character Pays

There are a number of ways in which contentment (peace) helps my finances. When money is low, the tendency is to be agitated and upset. This lack of peace and inner turmoil will make it difficult to hear from God and have timely direction when it comes to my finances; which career path, which job or business, what to do now, etc. The peace of God (contentment) will guard my heart and mind (Philippians 4:7) during this time. The environment of peace will make it easier to discern the path God wants me to take. The New English Translation and the New American Standard Version both shed interesting light on verse 6:

> *Godliness combined with contentment brings great profit…*
> I Timothy 6:6, NET

> *But godliness actually is a means of great gain, when accompanied by contentment…*
> I Timothy 6:6, NAS

I want to share a delightful story with you about how allowing the peace of God to silence the voice of material lust will pay major dividends. A man who worked as a pharmacist in a small community had bought a building lot where he and his wife were going to build their dream home. This particular lot was the only one available in the area which would accommodate the dimensions of their house plan. It took most of their savings to make the purchase.

One day he began to sense the Lord speaking to him about selling their lot. In a few days he concluded that indeed this was the Lord's will. He said, "Okay Lord, but first you need to tell my wife!" (Smart man.) A few days later at dinner his wife relates how she is sensing the Lord wants them to sell the lot. With this confirmation, the lot was placed up for sale. I know this must have been a hard decision, but this couple had financial peace and they could deny the voice of material lust (mammon).

The lot sold quickly and they realized a couple thousand dollars profit. That seems like small compensation for giving up a chance to build your "dream home." I'm sure they were wondering why God would lead them to abandon this plan.

One week after closing on the lot, a sales rep walked into the pharmacy. He explained to this pharmacist how he had an opportunity to sell specialized hospital beds to an area nursing home. His dilemma was that he did not have an open account with the manufacturer and he would have to pay cash upon delivery. Medicare takes a few weeks to pay invoices and this gap made it impossible for him to complete a lucrative deal. He asked the brother in this story if he would front the money for purchase of the beds. In return he would receive half of the profits. This arrangement led to more and larger opportunities through the same sales rep. When I was speaking at his church he was waiting for a check in the amount of $350,000, the largest deal yet. This entire testimony would not have been possible if he had resisted selling the lot intended for his "dream home." I can see how godliness combined with contentment brings great profit!

Mammon or God

Jesus said we cannot serve God and mammon (Matthew 6:24). God has a voice through His Word and by His Spirit. Mammon too has a voice. You can count on it taking an opposite position to what God is saying to you about money. Christian maturity will teach us to tune into the voice of the Lord and to tune out the voice of mammon.

Consider the preceding story. As the Lord was leading the couple to sell a lot which would accommodate their dream home, mammon would have been squawking all kinds of things. It would have said not to sell because after all, God loves them and would want them to have a bigger house, etc. Their ability to tune into the mind of the Lord and tune out mammon turned out to be the greatest financial blessing of their life.

In the second point in verse 9—don't long to be rich—Paul builds on the first one. I can't remember ever hearing a teaching from this verse either. I had never taught from it myself. The verse seems to contradict another one written by Paul:

> *For you know the grace of our grace of our Lord Jesus Christ, that though He was rich, yet for your sakes He became poor, that you through His poverty might become rich…*
>
> II Corinthians 8:9

I can see why we would like this verse and ignore I Timothy 6:9. I am happy to report that these two verses are going the same direction; there is no dissent. It is possible for God to increase our finances without us craving to be rich.

The longing to be rich is desire carried too far. This craving to be rich distorts judgment and leads to bad decisions. It will pull its victim away from the skills or trade which have been fruitful and into schemes which are only empty promises. Get-rich-quick schemes feed on the longing to be rich. The longed for riches seldom materialize.

Several years ago I was staying in the home of a couple who had been blessed financially in their real estate development business. They had a beautiful house and a good standard of living. However, they were experiencing much financial pressure at the time. The husband had been dissatisfied with the fruits of his labor and business. He neglected his development business and began pursuing numerous get-rich-quick schemes. Their income went south and the pressure created one very unhappy wife. The longing to be rich pulled the husband away from his strengths and now the whole family was suffering.

The voice of mammon tells us that the way to get rich is to have an intense passion to be rich. It may tell us to set goals consistent with being rich. I suspect mammon may even quote some Bible verses slightly out of context to that end. However, the longing to be rich will not make you rich; it is apt to make you poor.

The biblical alternative to craving wealth is to aggressively steward the gifts and resources the Father has given to us. The goal is to develop God-given abilities to their highest level possible. Be the best you can be. As I become more valuable in the marketplace, there will be a natural increase in the income I experience. In addition, if I manage and invest wisely the money in my charge, I will also see a lift to my finances.

Solomon was asked by the Lord to name any gift he

desired. Solomon could have asked for anything, including fabulous riches. Instead he petitioned for wisdom and discernment which was granted. The Lord also bestowed the things he didn't request; riches, long life, and victory in battle. Here are the verses from I Kings 3:

> *5 At Gibeon the Lord appeared to Solomon in a dream by night; and God said, "Ask! What shall I give you?" 6 And Solomon said: "You have shown great mercy to Your servant David my father, because he walked before You in truth, in righteousness, and in uprightness of heart with You; You have continued this great kindness for him, and You have given him a son to sit on his throne, as [it] [is] this day. 7 Now, O Lord my God, You have made Your servant king instead of my father David, but I [am] a little child; I do not know [how] to go out or come in. 8 And Your servant [is] in the midst of Your people whom You have chosen, a great people, too numerous to be numbered or counted. 9 Therefore give to Your servant an understanding heart to judge Your people, For who is able to judge this great people of Yours?" 10 The speech pleased the Lord, that Solomon had asked this thing. 11 Then God said to him: "Because you have asked this thing, and have not asked long life for yourself, nor have asked riches for yourself, nor have asked the life of your enemies, but have asked for yourself understanding to discern justice, 12 behold I have done according to your words; see, I have given you a wise and understanding heart, so that there has not been anyone like you before you, nor shall any like you arise after you. 13 And I have also given you what you have not asked: both riches and honor, so that there shall not be anyone like you among the kings all your days."*

Longing to be rich will not make you rich. This is actually backwards from a biblical sense. In the Bible there is a picture of God insisting one of His own adopt a higher standard of living. We will talk more about that a little later.

Let me use this example. God wants to promote us, but are we called to promote ourselves? No, Jesus said that when we are invited to a social gathering, do not go to the most prominent place (Luke 14:7-11). He advised going to the least prominent place, making promotion inevitable. The lesson is that promoting yourself and longing for promotion will not secure promotion. Longing to be rich will not secure riches either.

Now let's touch on that third point; it's okay to be rich (I Timothy 6:17). Paul explained to Timothy how to minister to those Christians who were rich. There was no condemnation given, only admonitions. In the verse Paul states that God gives us things to *enjoy*. That is another way to talk about peace. **When you reach the place where you have nice things, you will need that same peace you experienced when your finances were tight.** That peace will permit you to enjoy those things without being guilt-ridden or becoming goofy.

Some may believe that when they finally have more money, peace will come. Not so. When folks have nice things, they can be constantly worried that someone may try to steal them. When you are rich, you will have some investments. Those investments may be in real estate or they may be financial instruments. Investments will fluctuate. When an investment swoons, you will need peace. This state requires the exact same peace as when your finances were tight. It is the same. Your finances may change, but the need for peace about our finances remains constant.

Paul went on to admonish those rich Christians to be generous in verse 18. He exhorted them to be as rich in generosity and good works as they were in money. Let's read what he said:

> *Let them do good, that they be rich in good works, ready to give, willing to share...*

I Timothy 6:18

In order for anyone, including the rich, to be generous it requires peace. Regardless of our financial state, it is impossible to release funds without a strong degree of peace.

When is the time to receive peace about your finances? Right now! Ask God to impart His supernatural peace into your heart concerning financial matters. Allow His peace to clear your head and prepare to make the best decisions you've ever made in your life!

CHAPTER 4

QUEASY ABOUT MONEY

I have been impressed over the past few years about the theological barriers which can hold people back when it comes to money. Even though the person may be versed in the multitude of financial promises, there is a lingering thought that makes them uneasy about having more money. It is difficult for a responsible Christian to be comfortable about anything until we see Jesus as comfortable with the matter.

Church life has taught us to see the Lord as comfortable with spiritual things. We are fully at ease as long as Jesus is teaching and preaching. We are equally relaxed as He heals the sick and infirmed. Seeing Him deliver the oppressed does not disturb our tranquility. In all these situations we are both praising and cheering Him on.

There is something, however, which will unsettle us. Many would not be comfortable at the thought of Jesus making money. More specifically, we do not see Jesus being at ease with us making money. That unease can be a barrier to our financial progress. Until we see Jesus comfortable with us making money, we will not be fully relaxed with the prospect.

You see, there is a spiritual truth that we become what we "see" Jesus being. Check out this verse in I John 3:

> *2 Beloved, now we are children of God; and it has not yet been revealed what we shall be, but we know that when He is revealed, we shall be like Him, for we shall see Him as He is.*

At the Lord's coming we will be instantly transformed into His likeness because we will see Him as He is. That visual revelation will be overwhelming. Christian growth is similar, except at a much slower pace. Through the Word of God, and aided by the Holy Spirit, we progressively see a clearer picture of Jesus (John 16:16). We change into the picture that we see of Jesus. As we see Jesus comfortable with us actively making money, an internal battle is resolved and finances become easier. I believe the following New Testament story will be a great blessing to you.

Luke 5 is a wonderful place from which to teach finances. There are many directions a message could take. The route we will go today correlates to what I have said above. Let's read the first 11 verses from that chapter:

> *1 So it was, as the multitude pressed about Him to hear the word of God, that He stood by the Lake of Gennesaret, 2 and saw two boats standing by the lake; but the fishermen had gone from them and were washing [their] nets. 3 Then He got into one of the boats, which was Simon's, and asked him to put out a little from the land. And He sat down and taught the multitudes from the boat. 4 When He had stopped speaking, He said to Simon, "Launch out into the deep and let down your nets for a catch." 5 But Simon answered and said to Him, "Master, we have toiled all night and*

caught nothing, nevertheless at Your word I will let down the net." 6 And when they had done this, they caught a great number of fish, and their net was breaking. 7 So they signaled to [their] partners in the other boat to come and help them. And they came and filled both the boats, so that they began to sink. 8 When Simon Peter saw [it], he fell down at Jesus' knees, saying, "Depart from me, for I am a sinful man, O Lord!" 9 For he and all who were with him were astonished at the catch of fish which they had taken; 10 and so also [were] James and John, the sons of Zebedee, who were partners with Simon. And Jesus said to Simon, "Do not be afraid. From now on you will catch men." 11 So when they had brought their[were] James and John, the sons of Zebedee, who were partners with Simon. And Jesus said to Simon, "Do not be afraid. From now on you will catch men."

The first three verses find Jesus ministering to the multitude. He is teaching the Word, and perhaps ministering to the sick. This is a holy, anointed moment; lives are surely being transformed. We are fully at ease with all these happenings.

At a particular juncture, the Lord turns to Peter for the use of his boat. The use of his boat represents an offering. It is important to note that Simon Peter already had a relationship with Jesus, but now it is going to the next level. For more on that relationship, we need to look at some verses back in chapter 4:

31 Then He went down to Capernaum, a city of Galilee, and was teaching them on the Sabbaths. 32 And they were astonished at His teaching, for His word was with authority. 33 Now in the synagogue there was a man who had a spirit of an unclean

*demon. And he cried out with a loud voice, ³⁴ say-
ing, "Let [us] alone! What have we to do with You,
Jesus of Nazareth? Did You come to destroy us? I
know who You are—the Holy One of God!" ³⁵ But
Jesus rebuked him, saying, "Be quiet, and come out
of him!" And when the demon had thrown him in
[their] midst, it came out of him and did not hurt
him. ³⁶ Then they were all amazed and spoke among
themselves, "What a word this [is]! For with
authority and power He commands the unclean
spirits, and they come out." ³⁷ And the report about
Him went out into every place in the surrounding
region. ³⁸ Now He arose from the synagogue and
entered Simon's house. But Simon's wife's mother
was sick with a high fever, and they made request of
Him concerning her. ³⁹ So He stood over her and
rebuked the fever, and it left her. And immediately
she arose and served them.*

It is clear that there existed a developing connection
between the Lord and Simon. It is imperative that any
teaching or ministry about finance must be based on having a healthy relationship with Him. Biblical economics is
not a mechanical function. It thrives because of a healthy
spiritual life.

Let's look at how that association developed. From the
verses just above we gather that Peter heard Jesus teach in
the synagogue on more than one occasion. No doubt his
heart was warmed and comforted by the Word he
received. He was an eyewitness to the deliverance of a
demon-possessed man. He must have been awestruck at
the Lord's power and authority.

One Sabbath after service there is a new development.
Jesus drops by Peter's house for lunch! It is one thing to

relate to Jesus in the large group, it's quite another when He walks through the front door. Their relationship is taking on a new dimension. It is now one-on-one. The Lord can speak specifically into Peter's life.

Soon after Jesus walks through the door, He is aware that Peter's mother-in-law is extremely ill. He administers a healing so instantaneously that in moments she is up, helping to serve lunch! Peter is now a beholder of the Lord's healing power.

When the Lord asks Peter to give in Luke 5, it is a new chapter in their association. Previously the Lord has been doing the giving and Peter was doing the receiving. For the first time Peter gives something back to the Lord and he becomes a partner in Jesus' ministry. He is standing on a new plateau with the Lord.

Our tithes and offerings accomplish the same for us. Through them we become an active partner in the kingdom of God. It is possible to have the type of relationship where the Father does the giving and we do the receiving, but that is going to be shallow. A vibrant situation means the Lord pours much in and we return a portion back. He pours in the fullness of His nature and we return a small amount back through praise and worship. He sends us finances and we return a portion to Him via tithes and offerings.

Peter's giving sets in motion one of the biggest days financially he has ever had. It is always appropriate to evaluate what his motives were in giving his gift to the Lord. People can give for several reasons and not all of them are blessed. The overall basis for his giving is his growing connection to Jesus. He is doing it because the Lord asked. Also, he has been a firsthand witness to the miraculous power of Jesus. As he observes the crowd along the shore, he must have seen many needs. He knows if Jesus continues ministering, most, if not all, of those needs will be met. **Peter gives, not primarily for his own benefit, but for the benefit of those who need help from the Lord.**

That motivation is what the Scripture calls for in order for us to anticipate a harvest. Even the well-known Scripture on the tithe from Malachi 3:10 calls this to our attention. Take a look:

> *"Bring all the tithes into the storehouse, That there may be food in My house, And try Me now in this," Says the Lord of hosts, "If I will not open for you the windows of heaven And pour out for you [such] blessing That [there] [will] not [be] [room] enough [to] [receive] [it]."*

Malachi tells us to bring in the tithe, so that there will be food in God's house. The tithe is not primarily for our benefit, but rather for those who haven't had a harvest either spiritually or naturally. When the tithe is brought to the Lord with that motivation, it sets off powerful heavenly forces that will impact our finances.

As Peter watched Jesus minister from his boat, it must have been tremendously satisfying. His heart must have been warmed as he observed hope fill the eyes of those listening to Jesus. He probably forgot about the dismal catch from the night before and the bills pressing for payment. He is experiencing a holy, anointed moment.

Once that glorious event is wrapped up, Peter receives an unexpected benefit. In verse 4 Jesus tells Peter to go out on the lake and make some money! This command comes on the heels of one of the most precious, godly moments Simon has encountered. The proximity of these events presses our comfort level. One moment Jesus is preaching/teaching/healing, and the next finds Him telling Peter to go make some money.

Let me give you this illustration. Suppose that next Sunday your home church has the most anointed service in its history. The praise and worship reaches a level it has never been; your pastor preaches like a man from another world. Many have needs met at all levels. As your pastor dismisses the service, he does so with this exhortation; everybody go out this week and make a bunch of money! Everyone's comfort level would be seriously stretched; it would not fit the normal theological picture.

That is exactly what Jesus did with Peter. Some might feel He dropped from the spiritual (ministry) to the carnal (making money). Actually there was no change. It was just as spiritual for the Lord to tell Peter to make money as it was for Him to tell the sick to be made whole. There is no difference. Jesus was just as comfortable telling Peter to make money as He was under a heavy anointing. We should conform to that same comfort level when it comes to money.

Peter had a command: go catch fish! He accepts this mandate and proceeds to the deep part of the lake. He is empowered to fill both of his boats to overflowing; he doesn't have room enough to contain the catch. This solves the financial problem expressed in verse 5. Even though Peter left his boat to follow Jesus, Zacchaeus and the hired servants (Mark 1:20) will sell the fish and pay the bills. What a blessing!

It is interesting to note that as Peter went out to make money (catch fish), that Jesus went along in the boat. He is right there as they haul in that huge load. He sees the excitement in their faces as financial victory is snatched from the jaws of defeat. The Lord not only sent Peter out to make money, He went with him in the process. As you move into the workplace or marketplace, Jesus is right there commissioning you to make more money than you have ever made!

That's the Point

The abundant, miraculous catch of fish brought enormous freedom to Peter. When he indicated to the Lord his lack of a catch (Luke 5:5), Peter was not experiencing financial freedom. Jesus was preparing to summons him into personal service, but his financial bind would be a deterrent. Remember in chapter 4 we learned that Peter has a house, a family, and all the expenses that go along with those responsibilities. It would be dishonorable to leave them without addressing the financial needs. The fish that Zacchaeus will sell should pay the current bills and leave extra to take care of Peter's family for a few weeks, possibly a few months.

The overarching purpose for God blessing us financially is liberty. Financial liberty makes things possible that would have been impossible otherwise. Keeping that understanding in mind should help us to be more comfortable when the Lord speaks to our heart to make more money.

CHAPTER 5

THE AUTHORITY TO PROFIT

I t is normal to desire being profitable. It is also necessary. As believers we live in an orderly kingdom with principles. We are also under the reign of the kingdom head, Jesus Christ. We may find it difficult to profit unless God gives us the authority to do so. Because of the battle between the kingdoms, there will be opposition to us financially. **It is in the kingdom of darkness' best interest for us to be crippled financially.**

Our Heavenly Father is interested in giving us the necessary authority to profit. He can dispense that authority in a manner and at a time that pleases Him. Deuteronomy 8:18 is a verse which speaks of the Lord empowering His people to make some profit. Let's look at that verse:

> *"And you shall remember the Lord your God, for [it] [is] He who gives you power to get wealth, that He may establish His covenant which He swore to your fathers, as [it] [is] this day."*

The verse does not say that God gives us wealth. He gives us the power to obtain those funds. This sounds like a process and has overtones of spiritual growth. He remains in control of granting that authority or power.

Profit does not come naturally to most. It must be learned. Our Heavenly Father expresses His desire to teach us how in Isaiah 48:17:

> *Thus says the Lord, your Redeemer, The Holy One of Israel: "I [am] the Lord your God, Who teaches you to profit, Who leads you by the way you should go."*

Prodigally Speaking

The prodigal son is a story about personal growth and its relationship to making a profit. We can draw significant parallels between what he experienced and the growth we need in order to handle money on a larger scale. Read through the story from Luke 15:11-23:

> *Then He said: "A certain man had two sons. And the younger of them said to [his] father, 'Father, give me the portion of goods that falls [to] [me].' So he divided to them [his] livelihood. And not many days after, the younger son gathered all together, journeyed to a far country, and there wasted his possessions with prodigal living. But when he had spent all, there arose a severe famine in that land, and he began to be in want. Then he went and joined himself to a citizen of that country, and he sent him into his fields to feed swine. And he would gladly have filled his stomach with the pods that the swine ate, and no one gave him [anything]. But when he came to himself, he said, 'How many of my father's hired servants have bread enough and to spare, and I perish with hunger! I will arise and go to my father, and will say to him, "Father, I have sinned against heaven and before you, and I am no longer worthy to be called your son.*

Make me like one of your hired servants."' And he arose and came to his father. But when he was still a great way off, his father saw him and had compassion, and ran and fell on his neck and kissed him. And the son said to him, 'Father, I have sinned against heaven and in your sight, and am no longer worthy to be called your son.' But the father said to his servants, 'Bring out the best robe and put [it] on him, and put a ring on his hand and sandals on [his] feet. And bring the fatted calf here and kill [it], and let us eat and be merry; for this my son was dead and is alive again; he was lost and is found.' And they began to be merry."

The prodigal knows he is in the right family. He would certainly know that his father and the family have significant assets. He would likely be lacking a frame of reference as to how those assets should best be used. He may not appreciate the effort and stewardship it took for those resources to be assembled.

We also are in the right family, the family of God. Our Father has unlimited assets. As a matter of fact, the Word of God says that He owns everything. Psalm 24:1 reads:

The earth [is] the Lord's, and all its fullness, The world and those who dwell therein.

It is understandable that as a new Christian we may not appreciate exactly what it means for our Heavenly Father to have such enormous assets. We may not comprehend how any of that relates to us. This is an exciting discovery that comes as we grow in Christ.

The prodigal's father no doubt had a vision for what his son could become. He may have seen his younger son growing to take his place in the family business and estate.

The image of that alone gave him great satisfaction. The future reality would be even more pleasing.

An unexpected turn of events shattered this father's dream. The younger son began to express impulses not compatible with the father's vision. He voiced a get-rich-quick mentality and in verse 12 he demands his entire inheritance at once.

This episode must have pained the prodigal's father. He knew that wealth was not designed to be used in this way. He also knew his son's tendencies and that such a quick infusion of wealth would be a detriment to him. The vision would be delayed.

The behavior of the prodigal is a bit puzzling. He had not been denied the necessities of life growing up. His every need had been met throughout childhood. Something, however, stirred his craving for the "good life." The young man had an illusion, not a vision.

The prodigal may have been discontented at his father's slow pace. He may not have understood why his father didn't opt for a more lavish lifestyle. After all, the family could afford it. This attitude left the prodigal out of sync with his father and could be why the father hesitated at moving fast financially with this son. It set the stage for the next event.

The prodigal packs his things and heads toward the world. The excess money allowed him to separate himself from his father. Undeveloped character plus a wrong vision and a lot of money set the stage for disaster.

The young man entered into circumstances he was unprepared to deal with. He finds out that sin and loose living are very expensive. At every turn there were sharks waiting to cheat him. Even more serious financially is his inability to earn a profit without his father's supervision. In time, all of the inheritance money is gone.

The prodigal sinks to the next level. He takes the only employment he can find: feeding swine. The cruelty of the world confronts him as we learn that no one gave him anything (v. 16). Being away from his father and indulging in loose living left him without any favor. We don't know how long it took, but v. 17 tells us he came to his senses. We can see that something is happening in his heart. His mindset is changing. Attitudes are melting away. Something internally is being repaired.

Financial turnaround does not start in our checkbook; it begins in our heart! These changes may be a matter of our vision becoming like our Heavenly Father's. It may involve us turning from a character flaw. Before our finances can be fixed, we have to be mended internally.

A number of years ago I was speaking in a church in the Midwest and in attendance was an extremely talented individual. In spite of his ability he was in very bad financial straits. Some inward matters were out of sync and there were personal issues that needed to be addressed. I spoke that night on why money flows to some people and away from others. A work of the Holy Spirit began in his heart and gradually improvement came to his finances. We remained friends over the years and about ten years after we first met he sold the majority of his company out for $500,000 and the part he retained provided a residual income of a few thousand dollars per month. The point is that something in him was mended; the change also showed up in his finances. That is what we are witnessing in the prodigal son.

Reading between the lines we would say that God is dealing with the prodigal. He expresses an attitude of repentance. Perhaps he has caught a glimpse of what his father was trying to teach all along. He is catching his father's vision.

He desires to return home and be given the level of a hired servant (v. 19). The father reaches out to the son and surpasses the stated desire of his son. Instead of making him a servant, he restores him to the place of a son. Here's an important point: when the prodigal's attitude and vision became like his father's, the father treated him better than he would have treated himself. Is there a parallel with us? I believe there is. As we drop our self will and focus on what the Lord is focused on, He will treat us better than we would treat ourselves!

Time spent away from his father left the prodigal with many needs. Immediately the father starts addressing those needs. Returning to his father's presence made it possible for his needs to be met. If we will walk with our Heavenly Father, He will meet our every physical need.

Among the items imparted right away was food and clothing. His time in the pig pen would have decimated his robe and sandals. Can you imagine the vile odor which lingered on those articles? It is likely the father had them burned. How wonderful those new sandals and robe must have been.

There is something the father imparted which did not address an immediate tangible need. Verse 22 says a ring was also given. This item would not meet a need like food or clothing. In the scripture a ring was a symbol of authority. Pharaoh gave Joseph a ring (Genesis 41:42) and it empowered him in Egypt. By receiving a ring, the prodigal has a new authority in the marketplace. The prodigal can engage in business on his dad's behalf. The ring lets him know (and everyone else) that his father's resources are behind him. The prodigal now has the authority necessary to make a profit.

The prodigal has matured. He has accepted the privileges and responsibilities of sonship. He has received the vision of his father. The prodigal desires to assist the family at large. His desire is to help expand the family's estate. This change of heart allows the father to trust the son with both authority and money.

I want to take a look at a New Testament passage which combines inheritance and maturity. The verses are Galatians 4:1-2:

> *Now I say [that] the heir, as long as he is a child, does not differ at all from a slave, though he is master of all, but is under guardians and stewards until the time appointed by the father.*

When the heir is young and immature, you cannot tell a significant difference between him and a servant. Both the heir and the servant are under the master of the house's authority. Both are provided for by the master. Once the heir matures however, you will notice a big difference between the two. The heir will take his place beside his father. He will have access to the family wealth and business. The father will count on him to make a profit for the family estate. The family money will back him. The servant will never have the same privileges.

Even though he is an heir, he is expected to mature. Verse 2 says the heir is under tutors until a time appointed by his father. When a level of maturity is reached, the heir will take his place!

The relevance of the verses from Galatians is that we are heirs of God and joint heirs with Jesus Christ (Romans 8:17). We are called to an inheritance, but there is also a call to maturity. **Our Heavenly Father knows the corrupting power of wealth and chooses to release it into a mature situation.**

We can learn a lot from the prodigal's journey. Ask yourself the following questions:

- Do you understand the Heavenly Father's vision for your life?
- Has His will become your will?
- Are your attitudes becoming more like His?

If the answers to the three above questions is yes, you are closer than you think to moving into the most profitable place you've known!

CHAPTER 6

A TALE OF TWO SIDES

T his chapter may seem insignificant at first reading, but it can actually have the quickest payoff of any in this book. It deals with a facet of stewardship which seems small, but is really large. Solomon said it's the "little foxes that spoil the vine" (Song of Solomon 2:15). If you will pay attention to the things contained in this chapter, and act accordingly, within a short period of time something good is going to happen for you financially. I didn't say you'd become a millionaire soon, I merely said that something good would happen.

This chapter draws from a parable that is rich in monetary instruction, the parable of the talents found in Matthew 25. I will be drawing again on this parable in chapter 8. The great thing about this parable is we actually get to observe individuals handling money and see the results. Let's look at that story now:

> *For the kingdom of heaven is like a man traveling to a far country, who called his own servants and delivered his goods to them. And to one he gave five talents, to another two, and to another one, to each according to his own ability; and immediately he went on a journey. Then he who had received the five*

talents went and traded with them, and made another five talents. And likewise he who had received two gained two more also. But he who had received one went and dug in the ground, and hid his lord's money. After a long time the lord of those servants came and settled accounts with them. So he who had received five talents came and brought five other talents, saying, "Lord, you delivered to me five talents; look, I have gained five more talents besides them." His lord said to him, "Well done, good and faithful servant; you were faithful over a few things, I will make you ruler over many things. Enter into the joy of your lord." He also who had received two talents came and said, "Lord, you delivered to me two talents; look, I have gained two more talents besides them." His lord said to him, "Well done, good and faithful servant; you have been faithful over a few things, I will make you ruler over many things. Enter into the joy of your lord." Then he who had received the one talent came and said, "Lord, I knew you to be a hard man, reaping where you have not sown, and gathering where you have not scattered seed. And I was afraid, and went and hid your talent in the ground. Look, there you have what is yours." But his lord answered and said to him, "You wicked and lazy servant, you knew that I reap where I have not sown, and gather where I have not scattered seed. So you ought to have deposited my money with the bankers, and at my coming I would have received back my own with interest. Therefore take the talent from him, and give it to him who has ten talents. For to everyone who has, more will be given, and he will have abundance; but from him who does not have, even what he has will be taken away."

Matthew 25:14-29

We have a wealthy master who takes some of his assets and entrusts the funds to three stewards. He provides five talents of silver to the first steward, two to the second, and one to the third. He has in mind for them to invest the money in a way which will increase his estate.

The first two stewards take the capital and invest well. Their skill and resourcefulness is rewarded by a doubling of those assets. The third steward chooses to bury the silver.

Their master returns from his journey and promptly calls them in for a report. Those first two stewards had quite a report to give. They explained how they had doubled their money, and were understandably excited. The master was equally excited and he expressed his enthusiasm in a tangible sense. He promised them a greater amount of resources to work with in the future. He declared them faithful with the small amount they'd been given and he was going to entrust them with a larger sum. Faithful, by the master's definition, is using whatever is available to us and increasing it.

The third steward had a different tale to tell. He confesses that he had buried his money in the ground. The master was irate and immediately removed that one talent of silver from him and gave it to the one who had the most. This steward had made a huge blunder financially.

Two Sides

We now see the two sides represented in this parable. One side has money added and the other position has money pulled away. Two stewards had their original amount increased and other had his initial stake removed. Which side of the equation do we want to be on? The answer is obvious; we desire the side where money can be added!

This outstanding parable of money management is trying to communicate something significant. What if a present day believer inadvertently imitated the steward who had money pulled away? Would it affect their finances in an adverse way? Would it disconnect some of their reaping from their sowing? I believe the answer to these questions is yes.

What exactly did the servant do which displeased his master and prompted him to pull away that money? He was entrusted with money and resources that by his own choice became non-productive. Non-productive means it did not increase in value, it didn't help anyone, nor did it produce any revenue. When we allow resources to become barren, we forfeit our stewardship and the blessing it brings.

Is there a possibility that you, like that steward, are burying resources that God has entrusted to you? Few people today would bury $1,000 in their backyard, but they may be performing the equivalent thereof. How so? We may possess things of value we once used or needed, but now our life has changed, and we no longer require those items. We have no foreseen usage for the stuff and probably will not utilize it before the second coming of Christ! The items in question are not increasing in value, nor are they adding benefit to our lives. After prayer, you may decide that your action is the equivalent of burying that resource. You may be doing exactly the same thing as the steward in these parables who buried the talent.

I am not referring to assets that add benefit to our lives. The dining room table and the couch are important for day-to-day living. If you have a rare coin, it may not be considered buried because it could be increasing in value.

If you have an antique, it too would not be counted. It is probably increasing in value and even decorating some part of your home, and so adds a benefit to your life. Rather, you have stowed something away with no foreseen usage. If you decide, by the mind of Christ, that you have some buried assets, I want to talk about the remedy.

The Remedy

We are going to a verse that must be "rightly divided." It is a verse that if applied incorrectly could "mess up" an individual's life. This can be seen in a verse from Luke 12:

> 33 *Sell what you have and give alms; provide yourselves money bags which do not grow old, a treasure in the heavens that does not fail, where no thief approaches nor moth destroys.*

Depending on how I present the verse, and the way you hear it, this verse could be used to inflict great harm. The harmful approach could be that if you have any type of possessions, they must be sold and the proceeds given as an offering. Once that process began there would be no stopping place. If you have a house you have to sell it and move into a tent. Of course then you'd have to sell the tent and move your family under a bridge. The scenario would continue until an individual was divested of every material possession.

I am happy to report that committed believers in the New Testament had material possessions. Zacchaeus in Luke 19:8 pledged to give half of his wealth to minister to the poor. He was allowed to keep the other half of his wealth and did so with the apparent approval of Jesus. The believers in Hebrews 10:34 had possessions which were stolen as a form of persecution. They held these possessions with a pure attitude. It is clear from these verses and others that New Testament believers did not understand they were to sell every single material possession. What was Jesus saying?

I believe the first place to look is at the items previously described. The material possessions we no longer use are prime candidates. One translation of Luke 12:33 says, "Sell what you have and keep on selling…." This rendering implies a lifestyle attitude. The goal of Christian stewardship is not to see how many attics and garages we can fill up with stuff. **The goal is for any asset in our possession to be productive.** Once an item becomes non-productive, we should examine how to transform it into a productive asset.

I encourage you to take this seriously. We are stewards and God has entrusted us with financial assets. If we imitate the slothful steward and handle those resources in a way that is equal to burial, we position ourselves to have money pulled away. If we reverse this and "unbury" certain items, we slip to the side where money gets added.

I ministered in Alaska on a couple of occasions a few years back. These two trips were six months apart and I went to the same city, but spoke in two different churches. A brother who had been in the first meeting also attended the second set of services. He passed along to me the following testimony.

During the first set of meetings I shared briefly about the harmful impact of technically burying resources. He related how that the Holy Spirit witnessed to him that he was acting like the slothful steward and had some things buried. A chain of events unfolded which moved him to the profitable side of that parable. Upon taking a little inventory, he determined that the old jeep setting beside his garage was the same as buried. This machine didn't run and needed transmission work. His plan was to fix it up *someday*, which had never arrived. He decided that the vehicle was the equivalent of buried and needed to be sold. Before he could make his desire to sell known, he received a call. The voice on the other end of the line asked if he would be willing to sell that old Jeep he owned. The sale was made and he now had several hundred dollars in hand. That money had been buried in a vehicle and could now be directed in a more profitable way.

Upon further reflection he concluded that a camper shell he owned was also buried. He had planned to someday fix it up and place it on his pickup. He advertised it for sale and obtained a few hundred dollars which he added to the money from the Jeep. His attention was then drawn to a hunting cabin he had on the backside of his acreage. This structure was meant for friends to stay a few days while hunting, but was unsuitable to live in. He invested the money from the Jeep and camper shell in the building. He upgraded the heating system and otherwise made it suitable as a rental unit. He preceded to rent it out for $400.00 per month. In the same general timeframe he was approached by a communications company. They offered $300.00 per month rental fee, long-term, for a 50 x 50 corner of his property. This was an additional financial blessing.

In summary, this individual had an increase of $700.00 per month in less than six months. This positive change did not come because of a raise or promotion. It did not arrive by being an investment genius. It was accomplished because this believer moved to the favorable side of the parable of the talents. That simple move set off some powerful things for him financially. If you will adapt the same principle in your situation, I believe that good things will transpire for your finances in a short period of time. This fundamental of stewardship is very, very potent.

If you sense that some resource you own is the same as buried, let me suggest three alternatives that would equal better stewardship. The option you choose will be based on the leading of the Lord. He will direct you as to what fits your need at this time.

First, you could liquidate the item(s) and give the money as an offering to the Lord. This is better stewardship than having unproductive assets. You would be planting financial seed for a future harvest and you would be meeting a need in the realm of the kingdom. Our Heavenly Father will not ask us to give every dime every time. There are two other routes you may take.

Second, you could give a portion of the proceeds as an offering to the Lord. After that you might use the rest to reduce debt. That action would likewise show an improved stewardship over doing nothing.

There is a third alternative. After making an offering to the Lord, the balance of that money can become the seed for your financial deliverance. Here is an excellent case study I heard listening to Christian financial advisor Larry Burkett. I retell it with his permission.

A missionary had been of the field for more than forty years. Knowing that he would face mandatory retirement someday, he started setting money aside into his denomination's retirement plan. He earned interest on this money over the years. When he reached retirement age, his annuity payment was set at $125 a month for the rest of his life.

In the 1940s or 1950s, someone might live on $125 a month. In the 1980s, however, $125 a month hardly pays the light bill. What would an individual in his mid-60s, facing mandatory retirement, do in that situation?

This missionary had the presence of mind to ask for help. He communicated his situation to Brother Burkett who questioned the missionary for areas of special knowledge. The missionary had accumulated a good deal of knowledge about Hummels—figurines made in Germany which are one of the top collectable items in the world. The missionary's study enabled him to know when a particular Hummel might be undervalued, etc.

"Go home, search through your storage shed, your garage, and your attic," said Brother Larry. "Anything you don't need, liquidate it, turn it into cash, and then call me back." The missionary complied and assembled $1,800. The next step? "Take out an ad in the paper that says, 'I buy Hummels.' Include your phone number." The information he accumulated over the years taught him how to recognize value in that area of investment. He took the $1,800 he had put together and bought the Hummels that in his estimation were undervalued.

The retired missionary, on further counsel next took out a new ad that said, "I sell Hummels." People interested in collecting Hummels phoned. He repeated this process over and over again. The finale of the story was that the retired missionary later experienced an adjusted gross income of $265,000 for a one-year period.

This testimony did not come to pass overnight; it probably took a few years to happen. It started slow and built up to that $265,000.

The resource was in the missionary's hand all the time. It had been buried, but became the seed for his financial deliverance. Similarly, the seed for your monetary freedom may already be in your hand, if applied differently.

I am excited about what this chapter can do for you on a personal level. If the Lord impresses you that you have something essentially buried, consider taking some action as outlined in this chapter. Good things will happen for you both naturally and spiritually. On the natural side, you will have cash in hand which can meet the most pressing financial need in your life. On the spiritual side, you will move to the side of the parable where money will be added. That is the best part!

We may be amazed at what we see as our eyes are opened. We may not realize the degree to which we have stockpiled some things. There could well be an unexpected amount of assets available to you.

I remember one farmer in Wisconsin. He said, "I was here on the farm and had all this junk laying around. I was planning to give it away or dispose of it. It didn't seem valuable, but my kids finally talked me into having an auction." He held an auction solely to get rid of these items that he had planned to give away. He said, "Would you believe that I ended up with $24,000?" He probably thought he had nothing to work with, yet all the while he was sitting on a sizable treasure.

Another Dimension

Throughout this chapter we have looked at the personal impact of our topic. Now I want to discuss it from a corporate scope. What impact can those "buried" items have in regards to our church fellowship?

I have seen groups of people catch a vision as to what

they can do together with those funds. One church body sold the items they no longer used and with the money finished a "Family Life Center" that needed 35,000 more dollars. In another situation, church members used the money to pay down the mortgage on the building. These kind of stories make me realize that within each church body there is enough money the same as buried to fund a medium size vision for that group. The funds can help complete a local project or could finance a strong missions project. Who knows what direction divine creativity might take us?

As I reflect on this, I suppose there is billions of dollars worth of stuff the same as buried in the hands of North American Christians. What if I was speaking to all of them at this moment and each one caught the vision of this chapter. In a few months there could be several billion additional dollars made available for kingdom work. Think of the shock wave that would be sent through the corridors of hell! Long delayed projects could be finished and millions of believers would move to the favorable side of the parable of the talents.

The second half of the last sentence is the most important benefit from this teaching. It is hard to imagine the impact of having millions of believers pulling money in their direction. Make sure you are one of them!

CHAPTER 7

CONNECTING THE REAPING TO THE SOWING

Perhaps the greatest financial promise in the Bible appears in the apostle Paul's letter to the Philippians in chapter 4 and verse 19. He wrote:

My God shall supply all your need according to His riches in glory by Christ Jesus.

Woven inside this wonderful promise is also a great challenge.

Everyone has a tangible need. Maybe your need is for employment. Perhaps your car resembles the old Gospel song and has "gone the last mile of the way." Possibly you live in a two-bedroom house, but as you "multiply and replenish the earth" (Genesis 1:28, KJV), your family could easily fill a four or five bedroom home.

An Exchange

God says He will do something about our needs. He promises to supply them with His riches in glory. Those riches are just as real, actually more real, than any need.

However, those riches are in a different dimension. He is saying, "I'll meet your need in the earthly realm with riches that are here in the heavenly realm." The believer's challenge is to draw riches from the heavenly sphere into the earthly one.

Suppose I am in Texas. My pocket contains a large roll of Canadian one hundred dollar bills. Feeling flush with cash, I invite several friends out for dinner. After they leave the restaurant, I proceed to pay the bill. There I discover a big problem: all of that Canadian cash cannot buy one Texan hamburger. The money is real, but it comes from another realm. I can only benefit if I exchange it first.

The same idea applies to God's riches in glory. They are real. However, they must be exchanged in order to be useful. I need to convert "riches in glory" into U.S. dollars (or the currency of your own country).

There is a scriptural exchange process. It consists of five sequences. This pattern is displayed several times throughout the Word of God. This action was the main vehicle for changing someone's financial situation. It allowed them, and will allow us, to exchange wealth from the spiritual domain into something tangible. It can lead to an abundant flow of financial provision. At this moment you are very close to doing better!

What We Thought He Promised

Many Christians are trying to believe God for what they thought He said. A common perception is that if I present to God my tithes and offerings, then one day all kinds of money will show up. When the windfall doesn't arrive, some feel guilty that their faith wasn't strong enough, and others feel that God has let them down. A breach is created which needs to be healed. Is there a more excellent way?

The Biblical Pattern of Increase

First, the Lord asks us to give. This should not surprise anyone. Jesus unashamedly asks his followers to give to Himself. He even asked for a little boy's lunch on one occasion (see John 6:9-11). **Jesus boldly will ask us to present back to Him a portion of what He has blessed us with. Jesus does so because He plans to do something benevolent with it.** With one boy's lunch, he fed a crowd of 5,000 people. With our gifts today, he likewise uses them for good.

Second, God opens the windows of heaven. The prophet Malachi says that once we present our tithe as well as offerings to the Lord, He opens the windows of heaven.

> *"Bring all the tithes into the storehouse, that there may be food in My house, and try Me now in this,"* says the Lord of hosts, *"if I will not open for you the windows of heaven and pour out for you such blessing that there will not be room enough to receive it."*
> Malachi 3:10

It may be impossible to fully understand the phrase, "windows of heaven." Perhaps something opens in my heart which allows me to hear God's voice more clearly than ever before. Or possibly more spiritual light can now come into my life, since a window lets light in. Whatever the case, the "windows of heaven" are now open and dynamic spiritual forces are activated because I gave.

Third, once that window opens, God speaks either "an

idea, a concept, an opportunity, or wisdom"[1] that fits my life perfectly. (We will examine this thought in greater detail later.)

Fourth, I act on that word. I must put it into motion, whether it is an idea, a concept, an opportunity, or wisdom.

Fifth, a flow of finances is released. More finances come into my life than anything I have experienced to date. This pattern moves financial favor towards me as never before.

A Snapshot of Malachi 3:10

The Bible illustrates this sequence of divinely inspired increase in Luke 5. It is really a demonstration of Malachi 3:10.

> *So it was, as the multitude pressed about Him to hear the word of God, that he stood by the Lake of Gennesaret, and saw two boats standing by the lake but the fishermen had gone from them and were washing their nets. Then He got into one of the boats which was Simon's, and asked him to put out a little from the land. And He sat down and taught the multitudes from the boat. Now when He had stopped speaking, He said to Simon, "Launch out into the deep and let down your nets for a catch." But Simon answered and said to Him, "Master we have toiled all night and caught nothing; nevertheless at Your*

---

1 I have adopted this phrase from the teachings of Larry Lea. His writings include *Could You Not Tarry One Hour* (Lake Mary, FL: Strang Communications, 1990); *Listen to God* (Lake Mary, FL: Strang Communications, 1990); *Highest Calling: Serving in the Royal Priesthood* (Lake Mary, FL: Strang Communications, 1991); and *Weapons of Warfare* (Lake Mary, FL: Strang Communications, 1989).

word I will let down the net." And when they had done this, they caught a great number of fish, and their net was breaking. So they signaled to their partners in the other boat to come and help them. And they came and filled both the boats, so that they began to sink

Luke 5:1-7

In this situation, Jesus is ministering to thousands of people. Everyone wants to get closer. They want to see and hear Him better. Some push through the crowd, bringing their sick children to Jesus. Finally, Jesus is pressed against the edge of the lake.

Jesus knew that in order to keep doing what He does best, He must have a platform. Because of that need, He turned to Simon. Jesus asked the man who would become the Apostle Peter to borrow his boat. He asked him for an offering. It was not a cash offering, but a tangible gift nonetheless.

It Makes a Difference

Any time giving is taught it is paramount that a discussion of motives be involved. If a person is motivated by the wrong reason, their seed or offering will be neutralized. We have already looked at Paul's words in I Corinthians 13:3, that goods given for reasons other than love will not produce a harvest.

So, what was Peter's incentive for giving Jesus the use of his boat? Had he recently been listening to a tape about the hundredfold return? Did he imagine he would be compensated 100 times the monetary value of his gift? Of course not!

Peter was inspired by his growing relationship with Jesus. He scans the shoreline and is impacted by all the needs. He knows that each person can be made whole by a little exposure to the ministry and anointing of Jesus. Peter gives the use of his boat not for his own gratification, but for the benefit of those on the shore.

The connection between giving and motives is all over the Bible. Even Malachi 3:10 makes the point. It defines the reason for bringing the tithe into the storehouse— "that there may be food in my house." We bring in those portions, not really for our advantage, but for those who need food spiritually and naturally. When such pure motivation is present in giving, that combination unleashes spiritual dynamics that will overcome our financial need!

Back to the Story

When Simon Peter gave Jesus use of his boat, he was bringing an offering to the storehouse. The boat was the best thing he had to offer and was one of his most valuable possessions. What better storehouse than the ministry of Jesus, who met people's physical and spiritual needs every day?

Peter engaged Malachi 3:10. The windows of heaven open on him. Those same windows are open for everyone who is faithful with their tithes and offerings.

So what should happen next? If you applied what some folks picture in their mind to this story, fish would start jumping in Peter's boat. Peter has given, and shouldn't money just sort of show up?

Instead, Jesus told Simon (v. 4) to let out his net in the

deep for a catch. This inspired word from God was that third sequence. The Lord was speaking to Peter an idea that fit his life. The insight was about fishing and *"happy coincidence"*—Peter was a fisherman! Its intent was to bring a harvest to Simon because of his investment in the ministry of Jesus.

The word *blessing* in Malachi 3:10 needs clarification. According to the Strong's Concordance, it primarily means "benediction."[2] "Bene" means "good" and "diction" is a term about words. Webster's Dictionary[3] defines benediction as "to speak well of." Therefore, God is making this promise: "I'll open the windows of heaven and pour out for you a *benediction*, i.e., I'll tell or show you something." Those words can and will change our income structure.

A Time for Action

Peter must now respond. Catching fish in the deep part represented a new concept. Fishermen on the Sea of Galilee typically fished at night and in the shallow part of the lake. That approach is probably how Peter had always fished. His friends no doubt fished in a similar way. It was possibly the only way they understood fishing.

They had no idea that someone could ever go to the deep part of the lake, in the daytime, and catch fish. Suddenly Peter's thinking shifts about the fishing business. A new horizon has opened up. Hopelessness has been replaced

---

2 #1293 in James Strong, *The Exhaustive Concordance of the Bible.* (Peabody, MA: Hendrickson Publishers, n.d.).

3 *Webster's Ninth New Collegiate Dictionary.* (Springfield, MA: Merriam-Webster, 1985).

with promise and potential. Peter gave, the windows opened, and God began pouring out a benediction. The phrase "pour out" tells me that God will start saying it and keep saying it. Those words are flowing through our spirit and come from a never-ending supply.

Listening for Your Benediction

Many are trying to believe God for what they thought He promised. It is easier, however, to believe Him for what He actually promised. He has specifically promised to deliver a word with the potential to change our financial situation.

One does not have to hear everything God is saying through that window. I need only one tiny fragment from that benediction to change my life financially. Each small slice can bring in more finances than anything I have experienced up to that point.

Having heard the benediction, what did Peter have to do next? He had to act on it. Peter says:

> *"Master, we have toiled all night and caught nothing; nevertheless at Your word I will let down the net." And when they had done this, they caught a great number of fish, and their net was breaking. So they signaled to their partners in the other boat to come help them. And they came and filled both the boats, so that they began to sink.*
>
> Luke 5:5-7

This is an exciting story! Peter takes out his first boat, and the nets go over the side. They hauled in huge loads of fish. He was probably stunned at their success. He completely filled his first boat. Peter becomes "Mr. Enthusiasm."

Peter knew how many pounds of fish his boat can hold. He also knew the value of these fish. Historically, fish caught on the Sea of Galilee were of such good quality that they were dried, salted, and exported all over the Roman Empire. Since this was Peter's business, he knew the current market price. Peter could be forgiven for crunching the numbers in his mind as he pulled in the fish.

Do you know what else he was excited about? He had another boat. Peter looked over the side of the first boat after it was full. He knew more fish were down there. The second boat arrived and it was filled too. Peter knows there are even more fish down there, but both boats are full. He did not have room enough to contain them. That's what Malachi said would happen. Peter's experience was a portrayal of the promise in Malachi 3:10

That's Not the Point

The miraculous catch of fish did not make Peter a millionaire; that's not the point anyway! It did, however, give Peter new liberty. In a few more verses the Lord is going to call Peter alongside Himself to be trained. It would be difficult for Peter to set aside his vocation while his boats are empty. Luke 4 reveals that Peter had a family depending on him and he is honor-bound to meet their needs.

The two boats full of fish will meet his family's needs for a few weeks and maybe a few months. Mark's account (1:20) of this story indicates that Zebedee and some hired servants were also present. They will take the massive harvest and sell it at the market. This will pay the bills and put some extra in the bank. Peter is now *free* to concentrate on God's bigger plan for his life.

The point of teaching on finances is not about bigger cars and houses. Those things are fine, but they are not the focus. The point is *freedom*! The benediction and any financial increase it generates will multiply my options. I can be of greater service to God and His kingdom.

Mix with Faith

This story about Simon Peter illustrates God's promise. When someone tithes and gives, the windows of heaven open, releasing a flow of words. It will be necessary for me to mix faith with that particular promise. Nothing I learn from God's Word will help me unless I add faith with it (Hebrews 4:2). I must then begin pulling life application from that benediction, aided by the Holy Spirit. My attitude and declaration will be steadfast: God has promised to tell me something, and I expect to see something at any moment.

The idea or concept God reveals will help us transcend the natural. The obstacle against Peter was an adverse condition which limited his daily catch. He was out of answers. The benediction from Jesus lifted him above his natural understanding and enabled him to catch an extraordinary amount. The fish in the deep had probably been available on other occasions; Peter simply had not known how to catch them. He was enabled to catch fish at a new place and a new time.

Do Christians lack money because so little of it exists? Of course not. All around us are abundant resources. We simply don't see how to tap into them. A benediction draws together our skills, abilities, and characteristics.

They are then focused in a meaningful direction and arranged in the right order. The abilities you *already possess* will begin producing more income than they do presently. We do not have to become someone we are not in order to do better financially.

There can also be a creative element involved. A divine benediction can create an ability in us or even pull a dormant one to the surface. God does give gifts to men. The possibilities are only as limited as the wisdom of God!

Faith in Action

I relish the following testimony; it comes from the days when I first shared these messages in the church I was pastoring. There was a man in the congregation who had no financial or educational advantages. His income was low, especially for a family of six.

He received the teaching about God giving you an idea that fits. He mixed faith with that promise. A few months later he asked to share a testimony during the Sunday morning service. He started by telling us that his income over the past two or three years had averaged $175 per week. This, of course, fell far short of meeting his family's needs. I will never forget his next comment, however: "But God has shown me something!"

Theologically speaking, he had seen a picture in the "open window of heaven." He described how that revelation had changed his income over the previous four weeks. One week he had made $500, in another he had earned $700, a subsequent week yielded $1000, and then one week he had gained $1500. His income went from an average of $175 per week to a range of $500-1500 per week. Are you ready for a shocker? The additional income came through the same occupation he already had! The idea God gave him took his present abilities, redirected them, and increased his income to that degree.

The brother had a business in which he would haul away junk and trash. If you needed something taken to the landfill, you would pay him a fee and he would carry it away. He did a lot of work with mechanic shops and body shops. In the picture God gave him, he saw himself dealing with those entities in a different way than before. He no longer would quote them a price for hauling off some junk. Instead, he would offer to haul off a pile of trash in exchange for other items which might be greater value than any cash price he might charge. By that one change his income saw that dramatic rise!

You might be asking why he didn't see to do that before. That is the same question we'll be asking ourselves six months from now. Why didn't we see that? The opportunity was there all the time. I hope you are catching a vision. You are so close to doing better than ever before!

Jacob Also Received a Benediction

Another instance of this principle occurred in the life of Jacob. Jacob grew up in an atmosphere of wealth. (Abraham, his grandfather, was quite wealthy. Isaac, his father, was probably wealthier than Abraham. The Bible says that Abraham gave all that he had to Isaac [see Genesis 25:5]. Then Isaac added to Abraham's fortune [Genesis 26:13].) However, Jacob had some character flaws and tried to speed up his inheritance, but his get-rich-quick scheme left him broke. We went through this in depth in a previous chapter. God's covenant required a removal of those obstacles before Jacob could walk in the blessings of Abraham.

Nevertheless, God met Jacob in that condition (Genesis 28). The visitation occurred not at Jacob's best, but at his worst. God specializes at making Himself known when someone deserves it the least. This special encounter yields a Holy Spirit-inspired dream. Here is his response:

> *Then Jacob made a vow, saying, "If God will be with me, and keep me in this way that I am going, and give me bread to eat and clothing to put on, so that I come back to my father's house in peace, then the Lord shall be my God. And this stone which I have set as a pillar shall be God's house, and of all that You give me I will surely give a tenth to You."*
>
> Genesis 28:20-22

Jacob made a threefold commitment to the Lord. The spiritual one, "The Lord will be my God." He included a commitment to a place of worship: "This stone…shall be God's house." Third, he offered the financial component of his vow: "All that You give me, I will surely give a tenth to You." Jacob is bringing upon himself the promise of Malachi that the windows of heaven will open.

Jacob's Benediction Came Through a Dream

At a later time, Jacob received another Spirit-inspired dream that gave him his benediction. Jacob worked for Laban in return for the privilege of marrying his daughters. Near the end of that obligation, Jacob had a second dream. It occurred during the events described in Genesis 30; he tells his wives of the dream in Genesis 31:

> *And it happened, at the time when the flocks conceived, that I lifted my eyes and saw in a dream, and behold, the rams which leaped upon the flocks were streaked, speckled, and gray-spotted. Then the Angel*

of God spoke to me in a dream, saying, "Jacob." And I said, "Here I am." And He said, "Lift your eyes now and see, all the rams which leap on the flocks are streaked, speckled, and gray-spotted; for I have seen all that Laban is doing to you. I am the God of Bethel, where you anointed the pillar and where you made a vow to Me. Now arise, get out of this land, and return to the land of your family."

Genesis 31:10-13

Because the windows of heaven were open, a benediction (good word) comes. It is no coincidence that God spoke to Jacob about sheep. He was a shepherd. Through the vehicle of a dream, God helped Jacob comprehend something that would greatly change his finances. He was now positioned to be blessed like Abraham and Isaac.

Jacob was given a whole new insight into the sheep business. The idea and strategy would cause a major transfer of wealth. God seemed to be showing Jacob some of the biological laws governing reproduction and heredity. He was also giving him a master plan for putting that information to work in a beneficial way. His response was to act on what he saw.

So he said, "What shall I give you?" And Jacob said, "You shall not give me anything. If you will do this thing for me, I will again feed and keep your flocks: Let me pass through all your flock today, removing from there all the speckled and spotted sheep, and all the brown ones among the lambs, and the spotted and speckled among the goats; and these shall be my wages."

Genesis 30:31-32

Notice which sheep Jacob negotiated for as wages.

Exactly the same ones he saw in the dream. He was putting into motion what he had seen.

> *Now Jacob took for himself rods of green poplar and of the almond and chestnut trees, peeled white strips in them, and exposed the white which was in the rods. And the rods which he had peeled, he set before the flocks in the gutters, in the watering troughs where the flocks came to drink, so that they should conceive when they came to drink. So the flocks conceived before the rods, and the flocks brought forth streaked, speckled, and spotted.*
>
> Genesis 30:37-39

In those days, white lambs were the most desirable. Laban had arranged with Jacob that every baby lamb born pure white would be Laban's. Every baby lamb born spotted, speckled or streaked would be Jacob's. Laban, however, made a deal with someone who had "inside information." Jacob utilized those rods and affected how the sheep interacted and reproduced. Every time those rods were placed near the watering troughs, the future baby lambs were born spotted, speckled, or streaked. Therefore, they belonged to Jacob.

> *Thus the man became exceedingly prosperous, and had large flocks, female and male servants, and camels and donkeys.*
>
> Genesis 30:43

Verses 37 through 43 take place over a six-year period. That fact also provides us with some insight. We are not looking for an instant change. Proverbs warns us many times against getting rich quickly. We merely seek to be headed in the right direction.

When Jacob received those first sheep from Laban, his net

worth immediately improved. He was not rich yet, but his wealth grew as those sheep had baby lambs. Those sheep had more baby lambs, and the process continued until Jacob's finances hit an exponential curve in only a few years. (An exponential curve is a line that starts rising gradually, and then curves in a rapid upward direction.) In six years Jacob went from earning wages, and meeting his basic needs, to becoming exceedingly prosperous. Jacob's experience and the above time frames are a great lesson to all believers.

Our finances can begin improving immediately. We need not wait years and years. Peter sowed in the morning and reaped in the afternoon. Jacob went from just earning wages to being called "exceeding prosperous" in only six years. Both men were aided by a divinely inspired idea. Our Heavenly Father is saying something to you right now which will begin changing your finances.

It Will Fit Your Life

I want to share a story with you from someone who belonged to the church I pastored. At the time I was only starting to learn a few of the things you are reading in this book. But some received the teaching so readily that there were good results in a short period of time.

This young man was in his mid-twenties and a carpenter by trade. He had no educational or financial advantages over anyone reading this book. He worked hard. He earned his hourly wages. He met his bills, but was not yet experiencing all he should in his finances.

Being a consistent tither, there was a flow of words coming to him through the windows of heaven. One day he heard a fragment of the benediction: "You need to build a skateboard park."

I marveled at how that wisdom fit his life. As a teen he had lived in the mountains. He and his friends would take their skateboards to the top of a mountain and ride them all the way down the mountain highway. So he had experience with skateboards and had a good idea of how to make the park exciting.

His personality also contained a magnetism that attracted teenagers. He liked them and enjoyed working with them. Being a carpenter he knew how to build the obstacle course, ramps, and other props. The ability to do these things himself saved hundreds to thousands of dollars, eliminating a deterrent to the project. Thus God, with one small idea, pulled together these disconnected elements of his life and arranged them in a better order. The park opened and in a few months more than 1,000 teenagers used the indoor skate park. Each paid monthly dues to be a member. There was additional income from the sale of refreshments, pads, helmets, skateboards, and shoes.

The park eventually served about 2,000 teenagers. In less than one year we saw a brother go from earning hourly wages to receiving a multi-thousand-dollar-per-month cash flow. The heavenly inspired concept released more finances into his life than anything he had experienced up to that point.

I want you to think about something from this testimony. One well-designed word from God took parts of his life that didn't seem either significant or related, and blended them together in a way that changed his financial picture. There are many elements in your life which may seem small and disconnected. However, one bit of wisdom from above can weave them together into something that yields notable amounts of income. I want to exhort you to release your faith by expecting God to show you something through that window of heaven which is open over you right now!

God always has a way of weaving in spiritual opportunities as well. We must not overlook that aspect. This young believer had an evangelistic call on his life. He was always trying to find ways to tell teenagers about Jesus. With the skateboard park, he had up to 2,000 teens coming to him, paying him money, while he told them about Jesus. I stand amazed at how this particular benediction drew together both the spiritual and the financial sides of life. The potential of a divine benediction is incredibly far-reaching.

Powerful Delivery Vehicles

This chapter has highlighted the role of a benediction in the biblical pattern of increase. In order to convey our benediction to us, God has several delivery vehicles waiting in the wings. The timing of delivery is in God's hands. My role is to exercise good stewardship and move my finances towards divine order. Then I am more ready to hear. Sometimes the delivery vehicle is an inward witness; sometimes it is the clear, discernible voice of the Holy Spirit. If necessary, God also has the vehicles of visions and dreams (Acts 2:17) to get His word to us.

I had the opportunity to minister in the church where a certain individual attended. This man is a tither and gives as generously as possible to the Lord's work. He purchased a set of my teaching tapes and reviewed them several times. He was intrigued by the fact that God literally gave Jacob a dream.

This brother was a real estate developer and at the time of this story, the area where he lived was in the midst of a financial downturn. One day God impressed upon him an internal picture affecting his vocation. It was so strong he compared it to Jacob's dream. In this picture he saw a soil map that had the city limits of his town drawn in the proper place. Later, in his office, he assembled soil maps and marked the city limits on them. Then, within those boundaries, he colored in each parcel that already had a building on it. Using another color he filled in each lot that was designated as a wetland. (This type of property cannot be developed without a special permit.) Upon completion, his enhanced soil map revealed the lots available for development inside the city limits. To his amazement there were relatively few left which could sustain development.

This God-given picture came to him during the time of Operation Desert Storm. The Army had deployed troops from a nearby military base, causing thousands of soldiers to ship out to the Middle East. Typically, such departures hit a local economy hard; real estate prices can drop significantly. This scenario occurred, making tracts of land available at an undervalued price. This brother purchased the right to buy, within a set time, most of the undeveloped tracts at the present low price.

In the meantime he took his map to the mayor and city council, who had voted against annexing more land into the city. When they saw how little property was available for development within the city, they soon annexed more. The first land they annexed was 600 acres that this man owned right outside of town. Immediately that property value increased by a factor of five.

My friend soon learned that the Army Corps of Engineers had an easement through the 600 acres to build a road. They wanted to build a road on the edge of the property, but the surveyors had forgotten to record the easement. As a result, he was able to require the Corps of Engineers to build the road down the middle of his property. He received a paved road with a sewer line underneath and sidewalks on both sides. This remarkable event saved him many thousands of dollars.

When Kuwait was liberated, the Army sent this division home at 120 percent strength, not the 80 percent at departure. The community now had thousands more soldiers than before. Previously the emotion of fear had driven real estate prices ridiculously low. Now the emotion of greed pushed prices very high. Cash flow for this brother went way up. The initial dream soon led to other opportunities.

Balancing Internal and External Prosperity

This testimony highlights how a benediction both fits our lives and leads to increase. It also demonstrates God's ability to deliver a word through various means. **God is no respecter of persons. He delights in giving good gifts to all His children.**

Why would God establish the pattern described in this chapter? He can dump large amounts of money on anyone He wants. I believe the answer shows God's concern for our ongoing maturity in Christ. What He says through those windows changes me on the inside first; then it flows out and starts changing me financially. That sequence enables me to stay in line with III John 2:

> Beloved, I pray that you may prosper in all things and be in health, just as your soul prospers.

The benediction that comes through the windows causes my soul to prosper. Then, as I put God's good word into motion, it causes me to prosper additionally on the outside. In this way, my external prosperity stays in balance with my internal prosperity.

Money has incredibly seductive power. The temptation to love money or trust in riches can corrupt a believer. For this reason, Christian are in a dangerous spot whenever their external income exceeds their internal prosperity. The tension between the two puts pressure on that person.

Perhaps you have been disillusioned because you have given wholeheartedly to God's work in the past but have not seen noticeable improvement in your financial condition. You need to forget those things that are behind. Today you can begin believing God for what He promised, not for what you thought He promised. Just as Jacob lifted his eyes and expected to see something (see Genesis 31:10), so you must anticipate that the Holy Spirit will communicate a benediction to you through all the different vehicles available to Him. You will see something that fits your life. It will start lifting you out of the place where you are. It will start releasing more finances into your life.

CHAPTER 8

HOW BIBLE CHARACTERS MULTIPLIED MONEY

Another Way

In the introduction I talked about understanding the ways of God. One of the main ways that biblical characters reaped is that God would bring an opportunity their way. The party involved would mix some money, usually a small amount, with the occasion and a profit would flow. This chapter will shed more light on that process.

One Tuesday morning found me preparing for the following Sunday's message. I had just finished teaching on why money flows to some people and away from others. While meditating on those messages, I realized that a person has only three choices with any excess money in their possession. This reality applies whether someone has $10 or $10,000. All three options are outlined in the parables of Jesus. The first is definitely to be avoided. The second, while better than the first, lacks the potential to bring the kind of increase the Bible says is possible. Both Old and

New Testament characters alike utilized the third alternative in order to provide some phenomenal returns.

The application works with money, such as the cash that might be in our checking or savings accounts. It also relates to other resources—items that could be turned into cash if we wanted to do so. I want you to consider some things from the "parable of the talents" in Matthew 25. Since a "talent" in the biblical sense referred to an amount of silver, this parable could correctly be called the "parable of the money." It is a divine treasure chest of revelation concerning the multiplication of money.

> *For the kingdom of heaven is like a man traveling to a far country, who called his own servants and delivered his goods to them. And to one he gave five talents, to another two, and to another one, to each according to his own ability; and immediately he went on a journey. Then he who had received the five talents went and traded with them, and made another five talents. And likewise he who had received two gained two more also. But he who had received one went and dug in the ground, and hid his lord's money. After a long time the lord of those servants came and settled accounts with them. So he who had received five talents came and brought five other talents, saying, "Lord, you delivered to me five talents; look, I have gained five more talents besides them." His lord said to him, "Well done, good and faithful servant; you were faithful over a few things, I will make you ruler over many things. Enter into the joy of your lord." He also who had received two talents came and said, "Lord, you delivered to me two talents; look, I have gained two more talents besides them." His lord said to him, "Well done, good and*

faithful servant; you have been faithful over a few things, I will make you ruler over many things. Enter into the joy of your lord." Then he who had received the one talent came and said, "Lord, I knew you to be a hard man, reaping where you have not sown, and gathering where you have not scattered seed. And I was afraid, and went and hid your talent in the ground. Look, there you have what is yours." But his lord answered and said to him, "You wicked and lazy servant, you knew that I reap where I have not sown, and gather where I have not scattered seed. So you ought to have deposited my money with the bankers, and at my coming I would have received back my own with interest. Therefore take the talent from him, and give it to him who has ten talents. For to everyone who has, more will be given, and he will have abundance; but from him who does not have, even what he has will be taken away."

Matthew 25:14-29

The wealthy master in this parable knows the importance of making a profit. He likely has made significant gains over the years. These were "his own servants" (verse 14), presumably taught by him. We can imagine he had shared his experiences with them as they watched him make money. Now he took some of his money, entrusted it to them, and expected them to make a profit. One of the stewards was given five "talents," a second received two talents, and the third obtained one talent. (A talent represents an amount or weight of silver; some footnotes suggest a talent is roughly equal to $1000). All of his reasons for assigning them a portion of money is not clear, but he definitely expected them to help expand his estate.

While the master was on a trip, the stewards who received the $5,000 and $2,000 doubled their master's money. This accomplishment is impressive, whether today or in Jesus' day. The one-talent steward merely dug a hole in the ground in order to bury it.

Three Choices Available with Money

This master, upon his return, gathered the stewards together for a full accounting. He was impressed with the efforts of the first two. They took a relatively small sum of money and doubled the amount. The master promised them a larger sum to work with the next time and they would have the chance to make even greater profits in the future. We find this promise in the Master's words, *"…you were faithful over a few things, I will make you ruler over many things."* This cycle could be repeated with ever larger portions of his estate.

The man who received one talent of silver came to the meeting, but he misunderstood his master. His attitude seemed: "Master, good news, I didn't lose any!" The master rebuked him, however, took the one talent from him, and gave it to the steward who had the most. He was then asked one simple question: "Why didn't you at least take the money I gave you and place it somewhere it could have earned interest?" The master believed it was better to earn something than to earn nothing. The master wasn't saying it was the most profitable thing the servant could have done, only better.

From this parable comes the only three alternatives we have for increasing the resources or money which is in our care. First, I can do the equivalent of burying my resources, just like the one-talent steward (verse 18). (We went over this thoroughly in a previous chapter.) The second path is slightly better. Interest can be earned on those funds (verse 27). The third alternative is worlds apart. It follows the spectacular example of the two who doubled the master's money: "Then he who had received the five talents went and traded with them, and made another five talents" (verse 16). The word "traded" may be a little unclear to us. The NIV translation says, "put his money to work." The Living Bible reads, "The man…began to buy and sell with it and soon earned another $5,000." Thus the final alternative for multiplying money is to use it in some fashion to buy and sell, either long-term or short-term.

As I saw these three options in my study that morning, many Bible stories flashed through my mind. I realized how common it was for godly people to use their money to buy and sell.

The master must have been diligent to teach over the years. He evidently knew how to recognize unseen value in certain kinds of assets. This skill could have been something he had taught his stewards. Perhaps the master had mentored them on how to recognize undervalued investments. (Undervalued assets are things whose price has been driven down by a combination of factors, usually temporary.) Conceivably he taught them how to recognize the impact of emotional forces in the marketplace. For example, fear pushes asset values to unsustainable lows and greed pushes them to unsustainable highs. Neither of these forces can have a permanent upper hand. Whatever the case, their investment strategy was sound, and the master gave them deserved praise upon receiving their return.

The Bible records a similar story in Luke 19. It contains

the same parable, except that the stakes are now higher.

> *Therefore He said: "A certain nobleman went into a far country to receive for himself a kingdom and to return. So he called ten of his servants, delivered to them ten minas, and said to them, 'Do business till I come.' But his citizens hated him, and sent a delegation after him, saying, 'We will not have this man to reign over us.' And so it was that when he returned, having received the kingdom, he then commanded these servants, to whom he had given the money, to be called to him, that he might know how much every man had gained by trading. Then came the first, saying, 'Master, your mina has earned ten minas.' And he said to him, 'Well done, good servant; because you were faithful in a very little, have authority over ten cities.' And the second came, saying, 'Master, your mina has earned five minas.' Likewise he said to him, 'You also be over five cities.' Then another came, saying, 'Master, here is your mina, which I have kept put away in a handkerchief. For I feared you, because you are an austere man. You collect what you did not deposit, and reap what you did not sow.' And he said to him, 'Out of your own mouth I will judge you, you wicked servant. You knew that I was an austere man, collecting what I did not deposit and reaping what I did not sow. Why then did you not put my money in the bank, that at my coming I might have collected it with interest?' And he said to those who stood by, 'Take the mina from him, and give it to him who has ten minas.' (But they said to him, 'Master, he has ten minas.') For I say to you, that to everyone who has will be given; and from him who does not have, even what he has will be taken away from him."*
>
> Luke 19:12-26

It is important to know what a *mina* is. It is not a small sum of money; it is the equivalent of 100 days' wages. The master multiplied their daily pay by 100 and gave them that amount of money. It is more than a third of a year's pay. If you were to multiply your daily wage by 100, that would be a *mina* to you.

Occupy

The King James Version of Luke 19:13 reads, "…occupy till I come." The word occupy has changed its meaning since the KJV was translated. The Greek word translated "occupy" was a business and commercial term.

The New American Standard Version translates verse 13 as, "Do business with this until I come back." The New International Version says, "Put this money to work." These are very helpful, but I like the Amplified Bible here. Its wording is the clearest of all, "Buy and sell with these while I go and return." Two of these stewards took this challenge to heart.

If the two double-their-money stewards in Matthew 25 were good, their counterparts in Luke 19 are great. I call them the financial superstars of the Bible. They multiplied the master's money tenfold and fivefold, respectively. That level of return almost sounds ungodly, but yet the master said, "Well done, my good servant" (verse 17).

In dollars and cents, suppose a *mina* was $10,000. The first servant was saying, "Your $10,000 has made $100,000 more." WOW!

A few years ago, a pastor from Arkansas shared a story that helped me relate to the scale of profit potential expressed in Luke 19. This minister had listened to a tape on which I taught from these parables. The insights helped set him at ease regarding a prior transaction. I see that the Holy Spirit is dealing with Christians about making money, but there is a disconnect because we are not comfortable with the process. Personally making a lot of money is troubling to some. We cannot be at ease about making money until we see that Jesus is at ease with the matter. One of the preceding chapters has already dealt with this in depth.

Now back to the story of the pastor from Arkansas. He happened upon a chance to buy 400,000 used bricks for 2 cents apiece. He made the purchase for a total outlay of $8,000. He told me, "Within a few months the Lord helped me sell every one of them for 20 cents apiece." He had turned $8,000 into $80,000—equaling a $72,000 profit. He made a ninefold profit, almost as much as the steward in chapter 19 of Luke.

Whenever you hear a story of this magnitude, please remember that dollar amounts are not important. In the Bible, the emphasis is on percent and not dollar amounts. According to the parable in Matthew 25, the stewards were rewarded based on the percent of return, not the dollar amount. Whether the steward started with two units or five units, the master was just as pleased. This applies to our startup capital. Whether we're talking about $8,000, $800, or $80, we must always come back to one central question. If the above individual had not done what he did, what were the alternatives?

If money is the equivalent of buried, there is no gain. Funds placed out for interest earn a small return. Interest is better than nothing, but it pales in comparison to the multiplication seen in the parables.

To Bury or Not to Bury

The example of this pastor shows the need to understand our choices when it comes to utilizing excess money. This book examines scriptural reasons for why money flows to some people and away from others. It speaks of making Spirit-directed changes to move from the wrong side to the right side of God's promises. Buried resources can serve to short-circuit those promises even though I am believing and am obedient as a giver. (We covered this extensively in chapter 6 and I don't want to be redundant.)

Earning Interest

The second alternative suggested through Jesus' parables is that of earning interest on our resources. Nowhere does the Bible suggest that it is sinful to earn reasonable interest on our money in the normal marketplace. There were Old Testament injunctions against charging interest to a poor brother who needed the money for necessities (see Leviticus 25:35-37, Deuteronomy 23:19-20). No doubt you will have money on occasion that you need to park somewhere temporarily. This may be due to a lack of time or because all the investments you understand are overvalued. A little interest is far better than no interest.

Interest rates today usually lack the potential to produce the kind of financial blessings the Bible says are possible. That "engine" simply won't run that fast. Take 1993, for example. The official inflation statistic was 2.6 percent. Suppose you could earn 3 percent on short-term money that year. Adjusted for inflation, your net gain would be 0.4 percent. After taxes, you might end up with less buying power than when you started. On short-term money, you can earn a negative rate of return. Translation: you lose money every day. That is a far cry from something "pressed down, shaken together, and running over" (Luke 6:38).

There is a Better Way

Jesus' parables present a third alternative. The master said, "Buy and sell with these while I go and return" (Luke 19:13, AMP). In order to experience maximum financial benefit, I must own assets that increase in value. I should only put money to work in areas that I understand. There will be moments that I will be helped by a special leading of the Holy Spirit. I must be perceptive, open to the Holy Spirit, and willing to apply the things I have learned.

For example, in the fall of 1992, most Christian economists were quite pessimistic. They advised listeners to divest themselves of any stocks or stock mutual funds before the fall presidential elections. By contrast, I began to feel in my heart that all major stock indexes would reach all-time highs in 1993. I came to believe that the Lord wanted me to shift my small retirement account from a very conservative approach to the most aggressive stock fund offered by my fund family. Placing that phone call took all the courage I could muster, but the results were very rewarding. When I left that aggressive fund in January, 1994, I had advanced by 70 percent on the money that I had invested only seventeen months earlier.

One of my favorite stories was told to me by a pastor in Kansas. (I like this example because it deals with a small amount of money.) A member of the congregation knew something about antique toys. He would go to a garage sale or an auction and, knowing what was undervalued, buy antique toys for $25 or $30 apiece. He had contacts with people who collected antique toys. They would then buy these items for $300 or $400 each, resulting in a ten-fold increase.

I know these amounts are small, but what were the alternatives with his extra money? If he buries that $25, he earns nothing. If he put the $25 out at interest of 3 percent, in one year's time he would have earned 75 cents. Granted, 75 cents is better than zero. However, it pales in comparison to $300 or $400.

Is This Spiritual?

I think we need to talk about something here. Some might feel that to discuss any process of making money is somehow unspiritual. I understand that kind of thinking. Perhaps we should consider an instance from the book of Jeremiah in chapter 32. Jeremiah is by all accounts a spiritual man. He is not just a prophet, but he is nicknamed the *weeping prophet*. Boy, now that is spiritual: not only does he prophesy, but he weeps at the same time! His experience not only illustrates a lesson about making money, but it demonstrates how a godly man can profit while remaining at a high spiritual level.

Jeremiah is instructed to buy a piece of land owned by his cousin (verses 6-9). The area is currently under siege by the Babylonian army which, of course, has depressed the value of real estate (fear is driving prices to an unsustainable low). Jeremiah buys the land for seventeen shekels (v. 9). He is then told by the Lord that in the future men will buy fields for money (v. 44). Jeremiah is being directed to look through the present situation and see on the other side. He is made aware that when the Babylonian army leaves, land will become valuable again. His parcel will then skyrocket in value which positions Jeremiah to make a large profit if desired. *We have a picture of a prophet making a profit.*

I like a testimony which comes from a man in Missouri who made his living as a carpenter. After hearing the teachings in this book, a mobile home came up for sale in his vicinity. For unknown reasons, the price at which it was offered was greatly under the value he saw in the property. The carpenter realized this bargain thanks to his knowledge of property values. He and his wife had little extra money to work with, but they remembered the parable of the talents. They remembered that the master said to his stewards, "I want you to buy and sell until I get back." They went to the bank and arranged to borrow the money to buy the mobile home. Within three weeks of the purchase, they sold the trailer house and realized a $10,000 profit. They used the proceeds to pay off the mortgage on their home and become debt-free. Their action opened up another avenue of income.

Some people reading this material will be able to put this chapter to work right away. I received a testimony from a brother in New Zealand which I think will bless you. He found this teaching material on our website. Within a few weeks he testified that he had made $2000 on a car deal and another $2000 on a motorcycle. The revelation was the trigger that set him loose.

I want to address a legitimate concern. The subject matter we are covering conjures up images of profiteering in life or death situations. That is a far cry from what we are dealing with here. It is true, however, that when you buy an undervalued asset you are providing needed liquidity to the marketplace. There are times when market forces change the value of normal, everyday items and a person may find they are holding a possession that has dropped in price. A buyer provides them relief and allows them to "reset" their financial situation. The liquidity they receive is more important than the amount of money they obtain and they can now resume making financial progress.

Practical Applications

If every believer will put the concepts in this chapter to work, the Body of Christ will enter a new realm financially. Some will see phenomenal results. More funds than ever will be available for kingdom work. Let's discuss some practical things to do with the extra money which you will have in the future. Remember, a day is coming in which your finances will pass the break even point!

First, invest in your own skills or business. Planned carefully, this process will produce a safe return in the quickest possible time. For instance, if you are certain that a particular piece of equipment could directly increase your income, then consider investing your money in this way. The risk here would be very low.

Second, you probably have money you want to put toward your later years. Most Christian economists recommend putting those funds into an IRA within a growth-stock mutual fund. These types of funds buy and sell the shares of the world's or the United States' most promising companies. Some of these types of funds have averaged between 15-18 percent over twenty to forty year periods. This subject deserves to be researched at your local library.

Third, make your home a profitable investment. In buying any future home, consider only those situations likely to appreciate in value over the next three to five years. A couple of nice gains on a home means that in the future, your family can be in a nicer home for no more than your present payment. Again, your local library can be a great resource.

Fourth, invest in other areas where you have the ability to recognize value.

In Summary

Everyone is at a different place both spiritually and financially. A few can step out with the information from this chapter and begin reaping profits. Others will allow this information to remain on file in their hearts. At a later date, the Lord will use it to bring in a bountiful harvest.

I close this chapter with several admonitions. These are vital if you ever intend to profit in the fashion described in this chapter.

First, as a way of increasing your ability, seek out those in your circle of Christian friends who have made money either "accidentally" or on purpose. Proverbs 13:20a says, "He who walks with wise men will be wise." Glean understanding from them. Find out how they knew certain assets were undervalued. By so doing you become a candidate for the master to put resources in your hands.

Second, allow God to work with you to build up a surplus. Liquidate any resources that are the equivalent of buried. **Discipline yourself to set aside money regularly, even if it is a small amount.** Believe God for resources to work with. Without any reserve, opportunity can knock on your door and you will not be able to answer.

Third, do not strive to get rich quick. Proverbs warns us

several times against such tactics. I propose this alternative: do a little better this year than you did last year. If every Christian did so, the increased tithes and offerings would have a significant impact on global worldwide evangelism.

As you move toward financial freedom, do not assume that you must struggle each step of the way. Enjoy the journey and the learning experiences it provides. Most of all, enjoy Jesus each and every day.

CHAPTER 9

THE POWER TO CREATE WEALTH

This chapter is a follow-up on the last one. The topic is so comprehensive that it cannot be adequately covered in one section.

We are looking in this book at the ways of God and how He works to connect our reaping with our sowing. In the first part of this chapter I will endeavor to explain more about one of those ways.

In the Bible, God would bring an opportunity across someone's path. The party would add some money to the situation and God would bless with a significant harvest. It almost seems as if there is something supernatural about a believer having a little extra money waiting for action!

In light of these Bible experiences, we can expect God to work in that manner with us. He is going to bring an opportunity our way; it will call for a little money to be invested. When this moment knocks, will we have some funds with which to answer? I have told you of a gentleman who was a banker who related the following story one evening after I had spoken in his church. He said that there were times when he could have "bought a dollar for fifty cents," but was unable to do so. He didn't have the funds to seize the chances which drifted his way. When a good steward has even a small pool of money to work with, God directs special situations his way.

The Power

An oft-used verse on finance is Deuteronomy 8:18:

> *And you shall remember the Lord your God, for [it] [is] He who gives you power to get wealth, that He may establish His covenant which He swore to your fathers, as [it] [is] this day.*

The verse says that God gives us the "power" to get wealth. The verse doesn't say that He gives wealth, rather the *power* to get wealth. The Hebrew word translated "power" is used several different ways in the King James Version. Let me give you some of the more significant ones: "strength," "power," "might," "force," "ability," "substance," "wealth"[1] (Strong's Concordance). The terms strength and power are the most frequent renderings, but I am intrigued by the terms *substance* and *wealth*. This verse could read that He gives us the *substance*, or *wealth* to make wealth.

Ultimately it is our Heavenly Father's responsibility to ensure that we have some working capital. Our responsibility is to not squander this resource. That is the role for godly restraint, budgeting, and overall wisdom in the handling of our money. It provides a positive vision for lowering our debt.

---

1 #1293 in James Strong, *The Exhaustive Concordance of the Bible.* (Peabody, MA: Hendrickson Publishers, n.d.).

I want to look again at a couple of situations where God brought opportunities across someone's path and they put money to work. There are lessons here for us.

I want to recall the incident in Jeremiah 32. We gleaned something from this story in the last chapter, but there is more to learn. Jeremiah bought a piece of ground at the Lord's instruction for seventeen shekels. *Thank God he had seventeen shekels!* If he had been broke, the chapter would have gone unwritten. Instead, we have a guy in the Bible who had spare money available and that sum becomes a prophetic, as well as financial, lesson for us. The Lord brought an opportunity Jeremiah's way, he mixed some money with it, and a harvest was reaped.

Is there an unwritten financial chapter in your life? How many times has there been a legitimate opportunity you could not seize upon due to a lack of funds? This should provide much needed incentive for us to set aside a little treasure. Here's a verse:

> *[There] [is] desirable treasure, And oil in the dwelling of the wise, But a foolish man squanders it.…*
>
> Proverbs 21:20

> *In the house of the wise are stores of choice food and oil, but a foolish man devours all he has…*
>
> Proverbs 21:20, NIV

It is pretty clear from Proverbs 21:20 the disadvantage to spending everything we make. People say they live from "paycheck to paycheck." This may be true, but it is necessary that we believe God to have something available for those moments of fortune.

Let's look at another compelling story. We will go through

it with a fine-tooth comb, as I believe some things will be eye-opening. It's found in II Kings 4:1-7:

> *A certain woman of the wives of the sons of the prophets cried out to Elisha, saying, "Your servant my husband is dead, and you know that your servant feared the Lord. And the creditor is coming to take my two sons to be his slaves." So Elisha said to her, "What shall I do for you? Tell me, what do you have in the house?" And she said, "Your maidservant has nothing in the house but a jar of oil." Then he said, "Go, borrow vessels from everywhere, from all your neighbors—empty vessels; do not gather just a few. "And when you have come in, you shall shut the door behind you and your sons; then pour it into all those vessels, and set aside the full ones." So she went from him and shut the door behind her and sons, who brought [the] [vessels] to her; and she poured [it] out. Now it came to pass, when the vessels were full, that she said to her son, "Bring me another vessel." And he said to her, "[There] [is] not another vessel." So the oil ceased. Then she came and told the man of God. And he said, "Go, sell the oil and pay your debt; and you [and] your sons live on the rest."*

This widow was living a financial nightmare. The bills were behind and the creditor was coming to repossess collateral: her sons! That is brutal!

The prophet (Elisha) was nearby and she appealed to him for help. The course of action he prescribed is eye opening. Imagine a woman in a similar situation today and the counsel she would probably receive. Many ministers who speak much on finances would say she needs to plant a seed to secure financial deliverance. This would be tremendous guidance if she had not been a giver. (A different widow ministered to by Elijah in I Kings 17 was instructed to give, as she had no seed in the ground, and was delivered from her trouble.) Because of her testimony we may conclude that she and her late husband had been givers. She already had seed in the ground but her reaping was incomplete. Many need to cultivate the grace of giving in their life, but giving does not solve every financial problem. Some financial problems need a different solution.

Elisha asks what she has in the house. He is checking to see if there is any capital available. The widow informs him of the jar of oil. That is some capital, but not enough. Elisha tells her to borrow every available vessel. He is expanding her capital base. She needs many containers to capture the flow.

This is such an important point. So many wonder when God is going to make the oil flow. If He did, they'd have nothing with which to catch the overflow, i.e. no capital base to work from. It isn't clear what would have happened if the widow had not had the oil on hand or if no vessels were available.

This story clearly illustrates the connection between the natural and the supernatural. The combination makes an explosive force for God. The supernatural part in this account includes special direction, miraculous increase of the oil, etc. The natural part includes having the oil in the first place and gathering extra vessels to contain the miracle flow. What is your "oil"? Where are your "vessels"?

A Fresh Look at the "Wealth of the Wicked"

We are familiar with the statement in Proverbs 13:22 about the wealth of the wicked being laid up for the righteous. It has conjured up images of immense wealth being removed from unbelievers and being deposited in the bank accounts of humble Christians. Perhaps, but I think there is another application which is more common in the scriptures and is very exciting in light of this chapter.

There are instances when a Biblical character had such favor on their life that unbelievers made available their "stored" resources for investment purposes. The favor on Joseph's life compelled Pharaoh to make his treasury available. Joseph used the resources to capture enormous profits. The stewards in Matthew 25 and Luke 19 were granted the use of someone else's funds. The widow was had such favor that she was able to borrow vessels from all over town.

Believe for and expect the favor of God to be on you. Even if you don't presently have any funds to work with, there is the option of even an unsaved person making their funds available for your use. Increase your ability. Grow in wisdom. Believe for favor. One moment of divine favor is worth a lifetime of labor.

Sign Posts from Matthew 25

I can see at least six basic lessons which stand out in the parables of Matthew 25 and Luke 19. Each one offers insight and encouragement as to our financial future.

First, our Master is successful and wants to teach us how to flourish as well. "Thus says the Lord, your Redeemer, the Holy One of Israel: 'I am the Lord your God, who teaches you to profit…'" (Isaiah 48:17). Our Heavenly Father wants to convey to us His nature and wisdom which will enable us to succeed in all areas of life.

Second, using money to buy and sell is a heavenly

approved way of increasing financially. God is not against it as long as I do not violate other divine principles along the way. For example, if I lied in order to achieve a gain, then such profit will not please God.

A third principle involves a Christian staying aware that he is a steward, not an owner. All money is the Lord's. If we make a profit, both it and the money are His. Remember the steward's comments in Luke 19:16, "Master, *your* (emphasis mine) mina has earned ten minas." The steward understood that ultimately it was his master's money and the profits were his too. It is not unreasonable to think that the steward received a raise for his outstanding efforts. Also, if I make a mistake and suffer a loss, all I have is still the Lord's. There is a parable in Matthew 18 which covers even a loss we incur with the Lord's money:

> 23 *Therefore the kingdom of heaven is like a certain king who wanted to settle accounts with his servants.* 24 *And when he had begun to settle accounts, one was brought to him who owed him ten thousand talents.* 25 *But as he was not able to pay, his master commanded that he be sold, with his wife and children and all that he had, and that payment be made.* 26 *The servant therefore fell down before him, saying, "Master, have patience with me, and I will pay you all."* 27 *Then the master of that servant was moved with compassion, released him, and forgave him the debt.*

Apparently a steward made some bad investment decisions and prices moved against him. His account was ten million dollars short. He pled for forgiveness and was forgiven in spite of the staggering loss. Compare this to the steward who buried his one talent of silver and had no loss. He was cast into the outer darkness. One loses ten million and is forgiven; the other loses nothing and is punished.

The one who lost huge did so trying to increase the master's estate. The one who lost no money didn't even try. The moral of the story is that if in trying to multiply our Heavenly Father's money, we make a mistake and suffer a loss, we can be forgiven. I am His steward.

Fourth, it is the master's responsibility to put something in a steward's hands with which to work. In the parables he took his money and placed it in their hands. He will show me assets already available or he will put some new resource in my hands.

Fifth, **my duty is to increase my expertise.** The master put money in the steward's hands, "to each according to his own ability" (Matthew 25:15). I do not need to attempt some investment opportunity by tomorrow morning. I do not have to act next month or even next year. Rather, my top priority is to sharpen my abilities. The more I increase these, the more attractive it becomes for the master to put something in my hands to work with.

Sixth, and finally, motives are important to God. When the steward reported, "Master, your *mina*…," we gain valuable insight into proper attitudes. He knew it was the master's money and that he was making profits for the master's use. His motive did not seem to focus on luxury or what he would get out of the deal. This servant differs noticeably from the farmer who made large profits, planned to build bigger barns, and then said to himself, "Soul, you have many goods laid up for many years to come" (see Luke 12:18-19). God's response to him was, "Fool! This night your soul will be required of you"

(Luke 12:20). What a far cry from, "Well done, good servant…" (Luke 19:17). Both made profit, but one was for the master's use.

Rules of the Trade

It is helpful to know some things the Bible says about trading. There are some guidelines which will both guide and guard us.

First, there is an insight found in Matthew 7:13-14 which talks about the few who find the straight and narrow way. The thought here is that we must be willing to do the opposite of the crowd, as the multitude is often wrong. I remember a pastor telling me about his beekeeping operation. The price of honey dipped to fifty cents a pound and many in the business were getting out, i.e. selling. The reason for the low price was that a foreign nation was suspected of "dumping" honey in the U.S. My friend started buying some excess bees and hives, etc. The Commerce Department eventually placed tariffs on the foreign honey and the price went to $1 per pound. Now, former beekeepers wanted to buy in again. My friend split his swarms and sold them along with some excess equipment, profiting nicely. When the crowd was selling, he was buying. When the crowd was buying, he was selling! It takes the wisdom of the Holy Spirit to move this way.

A second vital element concerns recognizing value. I want you to read the following passage which speaks of this:

> *Again, the kingdom of heaven is like treasure hidden in a field, which a man found and hid; and for joy over it he goes and sells all that he has and buys that field. Again, the kingdom of heaven is like a merchant*

seeking beautiful pearls: who, when he had found one
pearl of great price, went and sold all that he had and
bought it…

Matthew 13:44-46

The merchants in the parables saw something others did not. They knew the items were grossly undervalued and therefore sold *all* they had to buy one investment. Normally that is risky strategy, but not since they found such undervalued treasure. This is why we must increase our ability: it allows us to recognize extreme value plays.

A third rule is to diversify correctly. This almost seems the opposite of the second guideline above, which showed the merchants concentrating their money in one investment. If we do focus on one asset, we must have great insight and skill, as well as deep pockets. Generally it is wise to protect ourselves with appropriate diversification, i.e. don't put all your eggs in one basket. Consider some wisdom from Ecclesiastes 11:

> [1] *Cast your bread upon the waters, For you will find it after many days.* [2] *Give a serving to seven, and also to eight, For you do not know what evil will be on the earth.*

"Cast your bread upon the waters" is investment terminology. Solomon had experience buying horses and chariots in foreign lands (over the water) and then reselling them to heathen kings (I Kings 10:28, 29). His advice is not to give all your investment money to one merchant or captain. If pirates attack the ship, your money is gone. If a storm engulfs the boat, down goes your investment. Instead, split your money between seven or eight ships. If one is lost due to adverse circumstances, the profit from the other six or seven will compensate.

Summary

The above thoughts about putting our money to work are by no means comprehensive. They will help us to develop a framework which will guide our investment decisions. We have much more to learn and a lot of that will come by personal experience. I would challenge you to enjoy the process as you are not alone. When the Lord sent Peter out to make money in Luke 5:4, Jesus accompanied him. The Lord was an integral part of the adventure. He is in your boat too!

CHAPTER 10

FIVE KINDS OF INCOME

M ost folks have a two-lane road or street in front of their house that is sufficient for the amount of traffic which needs to pass through. Imagine, however, the congestion that would occur on that roadway if rush-hour traffic from an LA freeway were diverted down your street. Clearly a two-lane passage would not accommodate the volume.

That simple analogy is pretty close to what many believers attempt to do with the financial promises outlined in the Bible. They desire for our Heavenly Father to send the magnitude of those promises down only one avenue or type of income. We know He will push as much through that one channel as possible, but could our income be better if we opened up some additional avenues?

Most people only receive income through their job. That is one avenue, but not the only one. The scripture suggests at least five types of income. The purpose of this chapter is to stimulate our faith and encourage us to develop some of those extra streams. I have crossed the Mississippi River in central Minnesota and even that far north it is a significant river. However, it looks nothing like the mighty flow that empties into the Gulf of Mexico;

many streams have converged to make a colossus. May God help you to have an income stream that resembles that mighty river!

The Main Avenue

The first avenue of income is what we call labor: our job or vocation. This is the main source for most individuals and the cornerstone of God's financial plan for our life. It is important that we enhance this avenue and not frustrate ourselves. The world is filled with people who detest their job; a Christian comes from a whole different perspective.

Christians work for a higher motivation than the world does. Being in the workplace for a believer is virtually a *calling*; we are commanded to work (Ephesians 4:28) and God has promised to bless the work of our hands (Deuteronomy 28:12). Seeing your job as a divine appointment will change your workplace outlook.

Due Diligence

It almost goes without saying that a Christian has a responsibility to exhibit a high level of diligence. Diligence is defined as "sharp pointed" or "strict decision."[1] Multiple verses in Proverbs illustrate the connection between our patient persistence and our financial improvement. Here is a sample from Proverbs 10:

> *4 He who has a slack hand becomes poor, But the hand of the diligent makes rich.*

---

1 #2742 in James Strong, *The Exhaustive Concordance of the Bible.* (Peabody, MA: Hendrickson Publishers, n.d.).

132

This discussion of diligence leads me to comment on a mindset that afflicts some people and is unbecoming to a believer. The mindset says it is fine or even preferable to just barely get along. It may call it noble to have a vocation which does not compensate you adequately. This is inconsistent with New Testament teaching. Listen to what Paul said in Titus 3:

> *14 And let our [people] also learn to maintain good works, to [meet] urgent needs, that they may not be unfruitful.*

The Greek word translated "works" can be rendered as "occupations."[2] There is a duty on our part to maintain the best occupation or employment we possibly can. We should take any reasonable opportunity to improve our skills and become more valuable in the marketplace. Stewardship requires that we make ourselves as useful to society as possible.

A companion word to diligence is *industriousness*. Industriousness creates its own opportunity. A continual application of the trait will produce openings for an individual to improve their income. Notice this passage in I Kings 11:

> *28 The man Jeroboam [was] a mighty man of valor; and Solomon, seeing that the young man was industrious, made him the officer over all the labor force of the house of Joseph. 29 Now it happened at that time, when Jeroboam went out of Jerusalem, that the prophet Ahijah the Shilonite met him on the way; and he had clothed himself with a new garment, and the two [were] alone in the field. 30 Then Ahijah took hold*

---

2 #2041 in James Strong, *The Exhaustive Concordance of the Bible.* (Peabody, MA: Hendrickson Publishers, n.d.).

of the new garment that [was] on him, and tore it [into] twelve pieces. ³¹ And he said to Jeroboam, "Take for yourself ten pieces, for thus says the Lord, the God of Israel: 'Behold, I will tear the kingdom out of the hand of Solomon and will give ten tribes to you.

Jeroboam is promoted by Solomon due to *industriousness*. Actually, that is the only reason given for his elevation. We aren't told anything else. We know nothing of his prayer life or giving. This is the tremendous power of diligence!

If you are having difficulty finding employment, consider giving yourself away. You can at least keep your skills at a high level. If an employer you would like to work for is contemplating hiring you, offer to work a week for free. Such a seed will surely grow into a job somewhere. If you are employed presently, recommit yourself to what you are doing. It is honorable and God will promote you.

A Second Stream

Our second avenue of income may be called creativity and resourcefulness. These attributes are fed by the benediction we discussed in chapter 7. The benediction amplifies our labor and makes it more effective, bringing to the surface dormant skills and abilities. A new dimension comes to our effort.

Creativity and resourcefulness find a need and fill that vacuum. **We see that a key to increasing income is mastering servanthood.** The essence of servanthood is expressed in the following passage from Mark 10:

⁴⁵ "For even the Son of Man did not come to be served, but to serve, and to give His life a ransom for many."

The essence of the above verse can yield thousands upon thousands of dollars over your lifetime. It is the supreme verse about meeting legitimate needs. Make the sum and substance of this verse a vital part of your thinking. I want to share a story of how this precept can improve your financial status.

When I moved from a pastoral to a traveling ministry, I did so based on a need I saw. I asked myself this question; how can I best serve the Body of Christ at this time? Could I best serve by remaining in the pastorate and ignoring this other need? Or could I best serve by relinquishing that position to another and moving to meet a need that I was equipped to fill? I knew the answer to that question and I began the transition into a traveling ministry. As I began meeting that need, my income rose.

In my first few months of field/traveling ministry, I did not carry any tape sets available for purchase. I was focusing at the time on three or four core teachings which were impacting people financially, so my repertoire was purposely limited. My thinking was that anyone who desired taped copies could purchase them from their own church's audio department. A lady however pointed out a need I wasn't seeing. She said it took her church two weeks to duplicate tapes. She wanted to review the messages right away, plus she had some friends she wanted to share the teaching with as well. She stated that if I had some sets available she would purchase three or four of them. She declared there was a need and that I should do something about it. I quickly moved to make tape sets available from then on and as I moved to meet another legitimate need, my income increased.

A few months later I was in prayer preparing for a service that evening. The Lord witnessed to my heart that there were many people who needed good study material (books, tapes, etc.), but at that moment they could least afford them. I sensed He was directing me to make all of my books and tapes available for a suggested price. If someone was hard pressed, they could simply do their best toward the suggested price. If someone was extra blessed at the time, they perhaps would do a little extra and everything would balance out.

You see, people who are in a hard place financially cannot spend large amounts on teaching material, even though it may help them. This is a legitimate need and the Lord was helping me address that inadequacy. As I moved to meet that need, my income experienced some rise. People liked the offer. Those who couldn't do the full amount did what they could and this was a little extra income. Those who could do extra did so and this was an increase. The revenue from the book and tape table increased by offering material for what people could afford. I learned much from this about how **looking to meet needs can positively help our finances.**

A Third Layer

The third form of income is the avenue of buying and selling. I have covered this thoroughly in chapters eight and nine. It is unnecessary to cover this again. It may be beneficial to remind everyone that it is vitally important to stay with assets they understand. It is good to remember that this avenue may only open from time to time. Don't try to force something to take place.

Avenue Four

A fourth type of income could be called answers to prayer or miraculous provision. Human effort is minimal in light of this provision. God is working apart from other normal avenues. (Financial answers to prayer can come through one of the other avenues, of course.) The Scripture, both Old and New Testaments, contain examples of this variety of supply.

There are many thrilling examples in the Bible of our Heavenly Father miraculously meeting the monetary needs of His people. One very well known model of this can be found in I Kings 17 where Elijah is sent to help a widow and her son. Let's check out those verses:

8 Then the word of the Lord came to him, saying, 9 "Arise, go to Zarephath, which [belongs] to Sidon, and dwell there. See, I have commanded a widow there to provide for you." 10 So he arose and went to Zarephath. And when he came to the gate of the city, indeed a widow [was] there gathering sticks. And he called to her and said, "Please bring me a little water in a cup, that I may drink." 11 And as she was going to get [it], he called to her and said, "Please bring me a morsel of bread in your hand." 12 So she said, "As the Lord your God lives, I do not have bread, only a handful of flour in a bin, and a little oil in a jar; and see, I [am] gathering a couple of sticks that I may go in and prepare it for myself and my son, that we may eat it, and die." 13 And Elijah said to her, "Do not fear; go [and] do as you have said, but make me a small cake from it first, and bring [it] to me; and afterward make [some] for yourself and your son. 14 For thus says the Lord God of Israel: 'The bin of flour shall not be used up, nor shall the jar of oil run dry, until the day the Lord sends rain on the earth.'"

This widow is in dire straits due to the famine afflicting the region. Elijah calls on her for a gift of food and water. It seems this widow needed to get a seed in the ground. Her generosity to the prophet ends up saving both her and her son. Sometimes the one thing that stands between us and oblivion is Spirit-inspired giving. (Giving of course is not the only answer to financial need. Elisha ministered to a widow in II Kings 4 who was already a giver, but needed a money making strategy.)

The miracle working power of God multiplies the barrel of meal and the cruse of oil. The food supply is stretched enough to last through the remainder of the drought. This provision required little or no effort on the widow's part. God was looking out for her in an extraordinary manner.

Here is a New Testament example in the life of Peter. During his time with Jesus a question of tax liability arose. In the scenario of Matthew 17:24-27, Jesus tells Peter to remove a coin from the mouth of the first fish he catches and use it to pay the taxes.

Peter's contribution is small compared to the supernatural element of finding that money.

We all can have a situation where we need some immediate provision that is beyond our present ability. Our Heavenly Father has come through for men and women in the scripture many times. Stay in the presence of God and be full of the Word. This preparation sets the stage for the supernatural intervention of God.

A Fifth Stream

A fifth sort of funds is inheritance. It is within God's plan for wealth to be passed from one generation to the next.

This is seen early in Scripture when Abraham passed a financial inheritance to Isaac (Genesis 25:5).

Inheritance is something that will happen only once or twice in your life. It is not a main source of income and is unpredictable in nature. You do not know exactly the time it will come your way. It is not something we desire to be expedited. When it does come, it can be a real help. Apply the same wisdom to that money as you would to your normal income.

A good way to honor your parents is to use an inheritance to make the life of their grandchildren better. This would be immensely satisfying to those leaving the estate.

Perhaps the best "inheritance" we can leave our children is to teach them that there is a way to go through life with either low debt or no debt. These life lessons will save them thousands of dollars and will impact them more than any inherited dollars.

You may be someone whose parents will not be leaving you any financial inheritance. I would encourage you to remember that in Christ we have obtained an inheritance spiritually and otherwise (Ephesians 1:11). You can look to Him to compensate for any shortcomings of your earthly parents. The Psalmist David said that when my father and mother forsake me, then the Lord will take me up (Psalm 27:10).

A Lesson on Income Streams

The virtuous woman in Proverbs 31:10-31 displays some skill in crafting multiple streams of income. Let's review those verses:

Who can find a virtuous wife? For her worth [is] far

above rubies. The heart of her husband safely trusts her; So he will have no lack of gain. She does him good and not evil All the days of her life. She seeks wool and flax, And willingly works with her hands. She is like the merchant ships, She brings her food from afar. She also rises while it is yet night, And provides food for her household, And a portion for her maidservants. She considers a field and buys it; From her profits she plants a vineyard. She girds herself with strength, And strengthens her arms. She perceives that her merchandise [is] good, And her lamp does not go out by night. She stretches out her hands to the distaff, And her hand holds the spindle. She extends her hand to the poor, Yes, she reaches out her hands to the needy. She is not afraid of snow for her household, For all her household [is] clothed with scarlet. She makes tapestry for herself; Her clothing [is] fine linen and purple. Her husband is known in the gates, When he sits among the elders of the land. She makes linen garments and sells [them], And supplies sashes for the merchants. Strength and honor [are] her clothing; She shall rejoice in time to come. She opens her mouth with wisdom, And on her tongue [is] the law of kindness. She watches over the ways of her household, And does not eat the bread of idleness. Her children rise up and call her blessed; Her husband [also], and he praises her: "Many daughters have done well, But you excel them all." Charm [is] deceitful and beauty [is] passing, But a woman [who] fears the Lord, she shall be praised. Give her of the fruit of her hands, And let her own works praise her in the gates.

The story is a collection of important facts and does not appear to be sequential. We get a picture of someone who is steady and progressively moves ahead. You do see an individual who is capable of generating significant income. Here are some of the elements of her success.

It is clear that the virtuous woman is a giver. Verse 20 explains her outreach to the poor. Giving and generosity are the foundation of a solid financial plan. As we saw in an earlier chapter, giving opens the windows of heaven. A fountain of creative ideas and energy is unleashed.

Some of that creativity goes toward a business venture. In verses 13 and 24 she develops garments for sale. This undertaking contains an important profile. It was low risk, fit her abilities, and took very little up front money. She is rewarded with success locally, but her garments are also finding a market in other places. The Hebrew word translated "merchants" in verse 24 means "Canaanite."[3] These foreign merchants were distributing her garments beyond a local setting. It provides an example of the wealth of the wicked being stored for the righteous (Proverbs 13:22). I want to mention a side thought. When wealth was transferred from the wicked to the righteous in the Bible, it mostly occurred through legitimate transactions in the marketplace. These transfers were in increments and not necessarily all at once. A massive and immediate infusion of funds can produce spiritual harm and not good. Increments are more healthy.

What else can we glean from the financial activity of the Proverbs 31 woman. She looks to expand her income. In verse 16 she buys a field and from her garment profits she plants a vineyard. She will be able to sell the grapes and the fruit of the vine. It is a second income stream. It is

3 #3669 in James Strong, *The Exhaustive Concordance of the Bible.* (Peabody, MA: Hendrickson Publishers, n.d.).

worth mentioning that she had allowed the profit from her garment sales to accumulate (v. 16). Having funds available is a very powerful tool.

Key Thoughts

The Proverbs 31 woman is a compelling story in many ways. Among the intrigue was her ability to generate money. We have much to gain if we follow her example. First and foremost, she was a giver. Her giving sparked creative ideas which fit her life and turned into a business. Let this example inspire you to be a great giver. Mix faith with your giving and believe God to show you something that will translate into an additional stream of income. She allowed her profits to pool up and it was investment capital which earned even more profits.

We have no hint of her following fads or get-rich-quick schemes. She had a clear vision for the path she needed to follow. Steady and diligent are words that come to mind. This is such a healthy example.

How can you benefit from this example? Be a generous, Spirit-led giver. Live under an open window of heaven with divine words and ideas streaming through your spirit. Allow those ideas to mature and raise your income.

Be patient and at peace. Avoid the ditch of "get-rich-quick" schemes. Walk in divine discipline when it comes to spending. Allow some money to pool up. Our Heavenly Father will direct opportunities your way to take advantage of that capital.

You are so very close to doing better financially. Now is the time to thank God for the changes that are coming to your life. I would be thrilled to hear the powerful testimonies that are going to flow from the insights you have picked up from this book. Please take a moment to write me as those great events unfold. I would count it an honor to rejoice with you!

A FINAL WORD

Dear friend in Christ,

It is my sincere hope that you have enjoyed the contents of this book. It is my earnest desire that the revelation contained herein will help you experience a financial turnaround. I would be thrilled to hear your testimony as it unfolds.

I am pursuing a vision to help the body of Christ connect their reaping to their sowing. You can play a part in this task. Please pass this book along to someone you know who will benefit. Feel free to teach from this book as opportunities make themselves available. Disciples are made as we teach others to teach others.

I would also ask that you would hold my ministry up in prayer. Your supplication will help me and this ministry to carry out the mission we have been handed. Also, please consider sending either a one-time or monthly gift to assist in retraining the body of Christ concerning finances. Your gift will go a long way in teaching others as you have been taught. The ministry address is below. Thank you and God bless. I look forward to hearing from you soon.

In Christ,

David Mallonee

Concepts in Stewardship
P.O. Box 207
Rogersville, MO 65742

www.conceptsinstewardship.org

144

Teaching Material from David Mallonee

Book(s)

Biblical Money Dynamics $15

Tapes/CD

Biblical Money Dynamics (10 tapes/CDs) $45

Building a Solid Financial Future (10 tapes/CDs) $45

Concepts in Stewardship
P.O. Box 207
Rogersville, MO 65742

For Visa/MC orders, visit our website:

www.conceptsinstewardship.org